Y0-BRH-011

CARL A. RUDISILL LIBRARY
LENOIR-RHYNE COLLEGE

The Golden Age of Colonial Culture

THOMAS J. WERTENBAKER

Edwards Professor of American History Emeritus, in Princeton University

GREAT SEAL BOOKS

A Division of Cornell University Press

ITHACA, NEW YORK

REPRINTED BY PERMISSION

CORNELL UNIVERSITY PRESS

First printing for Great Seal Books, 1959

Second printing, 1961

To My Wife
Sarah Marshall Wertenbaker

PRINTED IN THE UNITED STATES OF AMERICA

CONTENTS

CRUCIBLES OF CULTURE

THE American colonies produced no Shakespeare, no Michael Angelo, no Beethoven, no Pasteur; they could boast of no great accomplishment in music, or painting, or literature, or sculpture, or architecture; their only noted scientist was Benjamin Franklin. While Newton was discovering the laws of gravity, Harvey was studying the circulation of the blood, Milton, Jonson, Defoe, Pope, and others were writing their immortal works, Americans were busy chiefly with the axe, the hoe, and the saw. And this is as it should have been. The task which confronted them was not to make new contributions to civilization, but to extend its borders, to win for it a vast continent. A mighty task it was, a noble task, and right well was it accomplished.

The America of colonial days has been likened to a banquet, where the first comers, finding a feast awaiting them prepared by nature, had only to help themselves. It is true that theirs were the riches of a continent, but only on condition that they wrest it from stubborn Mother Nature. They had to risk the dangerous voyage across the ocean in the tiny vessels of the day, make their clearings in the forest, build their little cabins unaided by carpenters or bricklayers, put out their crops of wheat and corn, face the peril of the tomahawk, of hunger, of dreaded diseases. Their life was full of unremitting toil and severe hardships; it was not to be expected that they should create musical masterpieces or add to the world's knowledge of chemistry or botany. "No thing new and extraordinary in literature from this part of the world is to be expected," wrote Cadwallader Colden, "but as we are improving this wilderness and have in some measure in some places given it the appearance of cultivated grounds in Europe, so we make some small attempts for improvement in learning."[1]

And when the sturdy pioneer, resting after a day of strenuous labor, reflected upon the need for educating his children, he was faced with discouraging difficulties. He could unite with his nearest neighbors to build a crude schoolhouse, but their meager means might not suffice to secure a teacher, while within a five-mile radius were seldom more than a handful of boys and girls. There were no hard-surfaced roads in the colonial period, no school buses, and erudition often bogged down in the mud. Yet, even in Virginia and Maryland it was common to see children, hornbook and luncheon in hand, trudging through the woods or riding over the rolling roads to the "old-field" schoolhouse, while in New England, where most of the people lived in the agricultural villages, there was a really effective educational system.

As with the school child, so with the artist, the musician, the poet, the scientist. If one were interested in botany, one would have to pursue its study alone, with no stimulus from others of like interest save through an occasional letter. It required indomitable spirit and burning inspiration for a poet or an essayist to pursue his work amid the isolation of the forest or the tobacco fields. A William Byrd or a Robert Carter might surround himself with books, interest himself in music, architecture, and the classics, but he was not, could not be, a creative artist, scientist, or poet. It was only with the development of cultural centers, where men of like interests could meet to discuss the latest productions of Dr. Johnson, or the discoveries of Boyle, or the design of the restored St. Paul's

[1] Michael Kraus, *Intercolonial Aspects of American Culture* (New York: Columbia University Press, 1928), p. 126.

Cathedral, that the interest in cultural matters began to bear fruit.

With the growth of Boston, New York, Philadelphia, Annapolis, Williamsburg, Charleston, and other towns, came an increase in wealth which was all important for the development of intellectual and cultural interests. The day laborer, the field hand, the small merchant, the yeoman have neither the time to spare for music, art, and literature nor the means to indulge their fancies. It is only when one can build a beautiful residence that one's mind turns to the study of architecture; the ability to adorn a residence with family portraits creates an interest in painting and painters; the necessity of acquiring the polish and grace of the gentleman leads to a study of the classics and of current authors. The Boston merchant, the Virginia tobacco aristocrat, the rice millionaire of South Carolina, although by no means leading the life of leisure often ascribed to them, had the time and the inclination to turn from the counting room or the management of slaves or the disposing of crops to the higher things of life.

That this was clear to at least one great thinker of the colonial period is shown by Benjamin Franklin's plea for the founding of a college in Philadelphia, published in his *Pennsylvania Gazette* in 1749. "In the settling of new countries, the first care . . . must be to . . . secure the necessaries of life, this engrosses their attention and affords them little time to think of anything further. . . . Agriculture and mechanic arts were of the most immediate importance; the culture of minds by the finer arts and sciences was necessarily postponed to times of more wealth and leisure. Since these times are come . . . it is thought a proposal for establishing an Academy in this province will not now be deemed unreasonable."

Colonial culture, then, was crude in the seventeenth century under frontier conditions; it reached its full growth in the eighteenth century, especially in the decades just preceding the American Revolution. In these decades it was centered not in the newly settled Piedmont or the Appalachian valleys, but in the older communities of the East. It is true that the newer regions had distinctive cultures of their own—the peasant culture of the Pennsylvania Germans, the Scotch-Irish culture of the upper Valley of Virginia, southwest Pennsylvania, and elsewhere—but they were still crude, still hampered by frontier conditions. To these regions the refined East, with its cities, its colleges, its handsome churches, its gazettes, its theaters, was what England in the seventeenth century had been to Charleston or Annapolis or Boston. To the Lancaster farmer who halted his Conestoga wagon in the streets of Philadelphia to gaze at Christ Church, the building must have seemed the epitome of beauty and costliness; the Scotch-Irish delegate from Rockbridge who came to Williamsburg to take his seat in the House of Burgesses was struck with awe by the Capitol and the Palace and the Wren Building at William and Mary.

Americans have been slow to recognize the extent and importance of the culture of their ancestors of the colonial period. There have been apologies for the meagerness of the literary output, for the absence of great painters, the lack of distinctive American music, and little emphasis upon the excellent work done in architecture, the artistic crafts, and the widespread appreciation of cultural things—the drama, poetry, music, painting, the sciences. It is within the past few decades that R. T. H. Halsey and others have awakened our interest in old American highboys, tables, and sofas, in the beautiful work of Paul Revere and other silversmiths, in American pewter, in the correct proportions and quiet dignity of Mount

Pleasant at Philadelphia, or the Hammond House at Annapolis, or Drayton Hall near Charleston. Today, the thousands of visitors who wander through the quiet streets of the restored Williamsburg, visit the shop of the cabinetmaker or the silversmith, walk in the Palace gardens, view the handsome Georgian buildings, listen to eighteenth-century music produced by eighteenth-century instruments, have a new appreciation of the elegance, the good taste, the charm of colonial life in one of the chief centers of culture.

Culture in the colonies was shaped by the four great factors upon which all American civilization is based—foreign inheritance, local conditions, continued contact with Europe, and the melting pot.

The peoples who came to the shores of the New World brought with them the cultures of the Old. They continued in the American forests to speak the same languages, the same dialects, which they had spoken in Kent or Essex or Ulster or Switzerland or the Palatinate. They tried to establish schools and colleges modeled on those of the homelands, to erect houses just like those in which they had been born and had spent their youth, to wear clothes like those to which they were accustomed, to worship God after the tenets of their various faiths, to carry on the old industries and cultivate the soil after the European manner and with European tools. In short, colonial civilization was European civilization transplanted in the wilds of a new continent.

But this does not mean that each colonial culture had the same inheritance. We may speak broadly of European civilization, but we are conscious that there were many civilizations in Europe, many different cultures even in England. The immigrant who came from Devon spoke with a different accent from a Yorkshireman, was accustomed to a different type of rural cottage, possibly had different ideas of the proper way to worship God. But when settled side by side in Boston or Norfolk or Philadelphia, their differences seemed of minor importance when contrasted with those of the Scotch merchant next door or with the Huguenot silversmith down the street.

New England, more than the other colonies, had a uniform inheritance, for most of the settlers came from one class, having one religious faith, from one section of England. Yet we are reminded that they were not entirely East Anglians by such Devon, Cornwall, and Somerset place names as Plymouth, Barnstable, Exeter, Falmouth, Truro, and Taunton. Nor was East Anglia itself homogeneous in population, made up as it was of Anglo-Saxons, Danes, Flemings, and other elements. Yet the Puritans brought with them a well-established and distinct culture, which they planted upon the shores of Massachusetts Bay, with its Calvinistic faith, its East Anglian architecture, its modified manorial system, its dialect.

Very different were conditions in New York and the country tributary to it. Even in the days of crabbed Peter Stuyvesant, when the town was called New Amsterdam, it was peopled by a heterogeneous group, mostly Dutch, but also Walloons, Flemings, English, Huguenots, Germans. After Colonel Nicolls took possession for the Duke of York, English culture slowly superseded Dutch, but it was the process of a century. It is said that in the seventeenth century one might hear no less than eighteen languages spoken along the canal or on Coenties Slip. Thus the colonial culture of New York was a mixed culture with some of its main roots extending to England, others to the shores of the Zuider Zee, with minor roots in Flanders, France, and the Rhine Valley.

In the Philadelphia region the early inheritance, like that of

New England, was chiefly English, but unlike that of New England it was not drawn from any one part of England. Not only did Quakers flock to Pennsylvania from many English shires, but they were joined there by foreigners of similar faith–Dutch, Germans, Swiss, Welsh. And since William Penn made his colony an asylum for the oppressed of all peoples and all religions, it soon became a medley of races and religions. The farming country immediately around Philadelphia remained Quaker, the fertile belt of limestone soil stretching from the Lehigh Valley in a great arc to the Mason and Dixon's line was almost solidly German and Swiss, and all southwest Pennsylvania predominantly Scotch-Irish and Presbyterian. Philadelphia, itself, though newcomers of various faiths eventually outnumbered the original settlers there, remained under the cultural and political control of the Quaker aristocracy throughout the colonial period.

Further south, in the great tobacco region which extended from the Pennsylvania line to Albemarle Sound and from the eastern shore of the Chesapeake Bay to the Blue Ridge, the people were chiefly, although not exclusively, English. More than in any other region they represented various parts of England, various strata of English society, and various groups within the English Church. In Maryland and Virginia that Church was established by law and the great mass of the people were loyal to it, but it embraced within its congregations not only high church Anglicans but thousands of Puritans as well. Nor was the tobacco region entirely English, for there was a sprinkling of Scotch merchants, here and there a group of Huguenots or a pocket of Germans. In the main, however, its civilization was English, with its tongue, customs, architecture, and religion as unchanged as local conditions permitted.

Somewhat different was the situation in the rice and indigo region. The first group of settlers who set out for South Carolina under the patronage of Anthony Ashley-Cooper, later Earl of Shaftsbury, was a mixed company of English, Irish, and Welsh. Blown out of their course, they stopped at Barbados and took on additional settlers, the first of many from that island. In fact the migration from the Antilles grew to such proportions that Charleston was often regarded as a West Indian city. In 1680, however, two new streams set in, a stream of Huguenots fleeing the wrath of Louis XIV, and a stream of English dissenters who chose not to live in England under the Roman Catholic James. At the same time came Scotch Covenanters, Baptists from Massachusetts, a few Quakers, a few Irish Catholics, a large group of Dutch.

If the origins of different colonial cultures were diverse, the local conditions to which they were subjected and which changed them and molded them were more so. One wonders to what extent history would have been different had the Puritan fathers founded their Wilderness Zion on the banks of the Chesapeake Bay rather than in Massachusetts. Could they have established their towns amid the tobacco fields? Would their church system have disintegrated because of a sparseness of population, the great distances, and bad roads? Would a tobacco aristocracy have sprung up among them to dispute the leadership with the clergy? Whatever the answer to these questions, it is clear that the culture of colonial New England was profoundly affected by the soil, the climate, the harbors of the region; that Virginia and Maryland were shaped in large part by their great rivers, their mountain ranges, their rich soil; that South Carolina would have had a very different history had it not been for rice and indigo.

It was the rather sterile soil of New England which gave her a small farmer class instead of a planter aristocracy, her forests which made possible her shipbuilding industry, the great schools of cod and herring which made Gloucester, Salem, and Marblehead fishing centers; her many fine harbors stimulated trade and created her merchant aristocracy. This aristocracy it was which was so largely responsible for much of what is distinctive and charming in colonial New England culture.

In Philadelphia it was the broad Delaware, bringing the largest ocean ships to her wharves, together with the rich agricultural back country, which built up the merchant aristocracy. William Penn had planned a society of severe plainness, in which not only was the theater to be banned, but even music, costly furniture, and fine dress. But Quakerism could not prevent the development of a distinctive Philadelphia culture or even dictate its form. When John Adams visited the city to attend the Continental Congress, he found the Friends wearing their traditional plain clothes and broad-brimmed hats, yet dwelling in stately mansions, many of them filled with Chippendale furniture and elegant silver, and fitted out with libraries.[2] One traveler as he approached the city was surprised to see the suburbs "covered with villas, gardens and luxuriant orchards."[3] This region, like every other part of colonial America, could not escape the molding effect of local conditions.

In Virginia and Maryland some of the old families are fond of tracing their lineage back to the English gentry, yet nothing is clearer than the fact that the planter aristocracy was not part

[2] Charles F. Adams, *Works of John Adams* (Boston: Little, Brown and Company, 1850–1856), II, p. 395.

[3] R. R. Wilson, *Burnaby's Travels Through North America* (New York: Wessels and Bissell Company, 1904), p. 88.

of the English aristocracy transplanted to America. It was created in America, was the product of the rich soil, the vast network of inland waterways, and of the sunny climate which made the region suitable to the culture of tobacco, with slave labor and extensive methods of production; and this in turn created the wealth of a Burwell, a Byrd, a Carter, or a Wormeley. The Virginia aristocrat, despite his conscious imitation of the English squires, despite the tenacity with which he clung to English traditions, was not really an Englishman at all, but an American.

In the Carolina low country it was the character of the soil, the long and hot summers, and the inland waterways which favored the culture of rice and indigo, and rice and indigo were the chief factors in creating a highly cultured aristocracy, for they brought wealth not only to the planters, but to the merchants who traded from Charleston to Barbados and Antigua or across the Atlantic to England.

In Virginia and Maryland, also, the soil was the chief source of wealth, for it gave those colonies their staple tobacco. But there was no such alliance of planter and merchant in the Chesapeake Bay region as existed in Charleston, even though some of the most prominent families came originally from the merchant class. In the seventeenth century, it is true, we find Robert Beverley taking part in the slave trade and William Byrd I sending out his pack horses to the southwest for skins and furs, but gradually the tobacco planter confined himself chiefly to agriculture, leaving commerce to the English and Scotch merchants. This was perhaps inevitable since Norfolk, the chief mart of the province, was remote from the tobacco fields, was never the political and cultural capital, never became a refuge from malaria. The Virginia planter aristocrat, despite some family alliances, in time began to consider the merchants a somewhat inferior class and the mercantile pursuit not entirely in keeping with the character of a "gentleman."

The various colonial cultures, had they been able to shake off the dominance of the mother country, would have become more and more distinctive. The American regional architectures which had sprung into being in the seventeenth century in time would have become more American, more expressive of the life of Massachusetts, or Pennsylvania, or South Carolina. The American dialects would have grown less like the English dialects, less like each other. It is probable, even, that each region, had it been cut off from the works of contemporary English writers, would have developed a literature of its own.

But the colonies continued to look to England for guidance in cultural things and constantly reshaped their ideas in conformity with changes there. If in the mother country Chippendale furniture began to replace the tables and chairs of the Queen Anne style, it was certain that within a few years it would find its way also into the houses of the merchants of Boston and Philadelphia and the planters of Virginia and South Carolina. The lady who attended a ball in a gown outmoded in London, or who was unfamiliar with the latest English dance step, subjected herself to ridicule; the gentleman whose clothes were out of style, who had not read the latest English books, or who was unfamiliar with the gossip of the London coffee houses was considered behind the times. Thus while local conditions acted as a centrifugal force within the British Empire, the cultural dominance of England was a centripetal force, tending to prevent each section from flying off the orbit.

Although all the colonies were subject to the influence of

the mother country, it was especially strong in the tobacco region. Here the great fleets of tobacco ships which each year moved down from the rivers and creeks of Virginia and Maryland to the mouth of the Chesapeake Bay to head out through the Capes for England, returning a few months later with all kinds of manufactured goods, proved an iron link with the mother country. The planter, on his estate on the Potomac or the York, was in closer touch with London than with Philadelphia or Charleston, knew more of what was going on there. When the English ship drew up to his wharf he invited the master to dine with him, and, to the accompaniment of good food and rare wine, quizzed him upon the latest happenings at Court. This done, he would repair to his wharf to open his newly arrived crates and examine their precious contents—the latest books by Swift or Addison or Smollett, recent numbers of *The Spectator*, silver bowls, tankards, candlesticks for his dining-room cupboard, gowns, stockings, shoes for his wife and daughters, a set of new Chippendale chairs, kitchen utensils, farm implements, carpenter's tools.

In South Carolina, as well as in Virginia and Maryland, the cultural influence of England was strengthened by the Established Church, for a very large part of the ministers were English born and English educated. Not only did these men militate against the development of separate religious practices and tenets, but they constantly renewed and strengthened the cultural ties. Many added to their meager incomes by opening private schools or acting as tutors in the homes of the rich, and it was their influence in part which sent so many southern boys across the Atlantic to enter the English schools and universities.

In the northern colonies the tie with England was weaker. At the end of the seventeenth century, imports to New England from the mother country were about one eighth as large as those to Maryland and Virginia; in 1769, despite a considerable increase, less than a third. In fact, the commercial ties of this region were stronger with the West Indies than with England. If the wealthy Bostonian needed a silver teapot, he found Paul Revere and other Boston silversmiths quite capable of the finest workmanship; his clothes, his wig, his pewter dishes, his clocks, he could buy in the local shops as cheaply as from the importers.

New England was more independent, also, in religion and education. The Puritans, when they set up their Zion in the New World, claimed that it was the true Church of England, yet it differed from the established order not only when controlled by high churchmen, but by the reformers under the Commonwealth. The New Englanders set up their own colleges for the training of ministers and their own school system to prepare youths for them. Cotton Mather could boast that in its first century of existence New England had educated more ministers for England than England for New England. No doubt, Massachusetts and Connecticut kept in touch with the dissenting academies in the mother country, received inspiration from Philip Doddridge and other great educators, but on the whole they went their own way. Of the various "declarations of independence" which have gradually broken the ties between this country and England, the New England declaration of religious and educational independence was the first.

Nonetheless New England was by no means free from the cultural influence of England. The books which lined the walls in the minister's library were printed in England, most of them. Every educated man read his Tillotson, his Milton, and his Locke; the gazettes reprinted extracts from *The Spec-*

tator and *The Rambler*. The cabinetmaker who defied the changing styles in England and continued to make Queen Anne chairs after Chippendale had published his book of designs soon found himself without patrons. The simple four-square meetinghouses of the seventeenth century gave way to Wren churches; the plain residence with its overhang and dew drop, its central chimney and multiple gables, to the formal Georgian mansion. The tailor, or silversmith, or architect, or coachmaker who could boast that he had learned his trade in London regarded his American-trained rival with contempt.

Conditions in the Middle Colonies were similar. Both Philadelphia and New York developed groups of artistic craftsmen second to none in the excellence of their work, yet they followed submissively in the wake of the great English designers. Philadelphia discarded her early Quaker architecture, and New York her Dutch traditions, at the command of the Georgian school of architects. Princeton, the first college to be established in the Middle Colonies, was patterned after the Calvinist academies of the mother country. Yet here too there was greater cultural independence than in the South, for trade relations with England were less extensive and there were fewer English ministers and teachers.

4) Of the great forces which shaped colonial civilization, none was more important than the melting pot. Even though culture was predominantly English, though the mass of the people spoke the English language, read English books, accepted English styles, lived under English institutions, were ruled by English common law, the influence of foreign populations, religions, tongues, literature, agriculture, industry, customs, traditions was also great. At one time Benjamin Franklin expressed the fear that the Germans of Pennsylvania might im-

pose their culture upon the entire colony. "Few of their children . . . know English," he said. "They import many books from Germany, and of the six printing houses in the province, two are entirely German, two half German half English, and but two entirely English. . . . Unless the stream of importation could be turned from this to other colonies . . . they will soon [so] outnumber us that all the advantages we will have, will in my opinion, not be able to preserve our language."[4]

Although Franklin's fears proved groundless and the Germans of Pennsylvania, Maryland, Virginia, North Carolina, and elsewhere have either been absorbed into the population or are far advanced in the process, they have made deep imprints not only upon the culture of the regions where they settled but upon the nation. The colonies were much the richer for German thrift, German agricultural methods, German folk art, German craftsmanship, German music. The thousands of German barns scattered over southeastern Pennsylvania, western Maryland, the Valley of Virginia, and elsewhere remind us that there are still strong ties between the United States and central Europe.

The Scotch-Irish, more than the Germans, have melted into the population, yet they too have made invaluable contributions. Gone is the Scotch accent, gone the whirring bagpipe, gone even their skill as weavers, gone the quaint old costumes, the superstitions and customs, but their influence upon religion and education is attested today by thousands of Presbyterian congregations and scores of schools, colleges, and universities. For a century Princeton was the religious and educational capital of Scotch-Irish America, sending forth hundreds of ministers and teachers to southwestern Pennsylvania, Vir-

[4] Jared Sparks, *The Works of Benjamin Franklin* (Chicago: T. MacConn, 1882), VIII, pp. 71–73.

ginia, and North Carolina, and even to far-off Tennessee and Kentucky.

In New York the story is the same. When one visits lower Manhattan and wanders through the narrow streets beneath the towering buildings, he can hardly believe that for a century and a half a Dutch town occupied this space. New Amsterdam has vanished from the face of the earth. Yet the days of Peter Stuyvesant are brought back in imagination when we meet a Roosevelt or a Van Dyke or a Cowenhoven, when we walk along the Bowery or Cortlandt street, when we purchase a "cookie" or step over a "stoop" or read the latest baseball "dope." The distinctive Dutch haystack, with its sliding roof, is still in use in the farming regions of eastern New Jersey and southern New York; the Dutch barn can be recognized at a glance as different from the English barn or the German barn.

It is clear that colonial culture follows a very complex pattern. There was no one uniform culture, but a dozen or more; not only the cultures of New England, the Middle Colonies, and the South, but of subdivisions in these major sections. In the South alone one must differentiate between the tobacco region, the rice region, the mercantile region, the pine belt, and the great back country. In Pennsylvania the German and Swiss belt differed radically from the Quaker region, which in turn was quite unlike the Scotch-Irish southwest. Moreover, within these various districts different groups had different cultures; the life of the wealthy tobacco planter was different from that of the yeoman farmer nearby, that of the great merchant from that of the cabinetmaker a few doors down the street. Finally, seventeenth-century culture, when the colonies were still in the pioneer stage, was very different from the more sophisticated culture of the mid-eighteenth century.

Any consideration of colonial culture should make a sharp

distinction between creative work and mere interest in cultural things. Of the former comparatively little was done that was worth while, but the latter proved a powerful force in shaping the thought and life of the people. There was a colonial literature which reflects the spirit of the times, introduces us to the fears, the strivings, the joys, the sorrows of this interesting period. But it consists not of the dreary poetry of Urian Oakes or of Michael Wigglesworth, not of the sermons of the Puritan ministers, but of the letters of merchants, planters, officials, teachers, clergymen, of diaries, reports, and local histories. The *Journal* of the Reverend Robert Rose and the *Diary* of Judge Samuel Sewall are more revealing, are more interesting than a dozen poems.

Moreover, the culture of the period expressed itself not only in literature, but in architecture, music, the artistic crafts, the theater, and science. The wealthy man who pored over the pages of Gibbs's *A Book of Architecture* in quest of ideas for his own residence, who attended productions of *Othello* or *Macbeth* at Kean's Theater in New York or the old theater in Williamsburg, who experimented with foreign plants in his garden, who furnished his house with the exquisite tables and chairs of Thomas Affleck or William Savery, who enjoyed the music of Bach or Handel was doing his part in molding the cultural life of the colonies.

In the present volume we shall confine ourselves to the great centers of culture in the colonial east, ignoring the newer and cruder, but not less interesting, cultures of the back country. In these cultural centers the emphasis will be placed not on the seventeenth century, but upon the mid-eighteenth century, when a higher degree of refinement had been reached. The remaining six chapters will be devoted in succession to Boston, New York, Philadelphia, Annapolis, Williamsburg, and Charleston.

THE PURITAN BEGINS TO PLAY

Boston

WHEN Increase Mather was nearing his end he received a letter from a friend asking whether he were still in the land of the living. "No," he replied, "tell him I am going to it, this poor world is the land of the dying." Colonial Boston of the eighteenth century to the leaders of the old unbending Puritanism seemed a place of corruption, evil, and ungodliness. It was in vain that Cotton Mather wrote his *Magnalia* extolling the old clergy as prophets and likening the great exodus to the flight from Egypt, that the Calvinist ministers thundered from the pulpit their denunciations of all change, that the heavy hand of moral censure or even of the law fell on those who broke the old Puritan code. A liberal spirit was awake in the city of John Cotton, which insisted upon freedom of thought and conduct, saw no evil in theaters and concerts, was skeptical of Calvin's "burning" hell, repudiated the authority of the old "theocracy."

Cotton Mather often surprises us by his liberality in scientific matters, by his acceptance of the Copernican system, or his support of inoculation for smallpox, but he struck out with all his might against anything which tended to weaken the old order. The liberalizing of Harvard by John Leverett and Thomas and William Brattle was wormwood to him; he condemned the luxury which was growing apace; he warned against the playing of cards, the singing of ballads, the celebration of Christmas. And when he had finished his days the doubt creeps in

battle was carried on by his friend Samuel Sewall and others of the old school. Plays and music houses were forbidden; Sewall denounced the use of periwigs as unbiblical; and when some of the young people organized an assembly, it was frowned upon and the ladies who took part in it stigmatized as "none of the nicest in regard to their reputations."

Yet it was futile for the conservative group to set themselves against the trend of the times. The governors and other Crown officials built fine houses, filled them with costly furniture and silver, purchased coaches, surrounded themselves with liveried slaves, and many of the wealthy merchants followed their example. "Notwithstanding plays and such like diversions do not obtain here," wrote the traveler Bennett in 1740, "they don't seem to be dispirited nor moped for want of them, for both the ladies and gentlemen dress and appear as gay in common as courtiers in England. . . . The ladies here visit, drink tea and indulge every little piece of gentility to the height of the mode and neglect the affairs of their families with as good a grace as the finest ladies in London. . . . When the ladies ride out to take the air it is generally in a chaise or chair . . . and they have a negro servant to drive them."[1]

Save for the officials, most of whom were Church of England men, and a few immigrant families such as the Bowdoins and the Faneuils, the Boston aristocrats were of Puritan stock and adhered, though with slackened zeal, to the Congregational faith. Many had been touched with the liberal spirit, and, to the horror of the old clergy, actually flirted with Arminianism. One honest soul did not hesitate to defend his faith in the columns of the *Evening-Post*. "One would imagine . . . that God had promised Heaven only to Calvinists and pre-

[1] Bennett's "MSS. History of New England," Massachusetts Historical Society *Proceedings*, January 1861, pp. 124–126.

pared Hell for the Arminians," he wrote. "[Some preachers] . . . are perpetually thundering out Hell and damnation against Arminians, coupling them with the Devil."[2]

Worthy Peter Faneuil typified the more liberal group. We see him on Sundays, splendid in his snuff-brown velvet suit and full-bottomed wig, crossing the street from his residence to King's Chapel and entering to take his accustomed seat. His mansion he inherited from his uncle, Andrew Faneuil, and here he lived sumptuously with his Negro slaves, his silver plate, his coach and chariot, and his fine English horses. By his gift of Faneuil Hall, that cradle of liberty, he stamped his name indelibly on the pages of American history.[3]

It was commerce which was largely responsible for the profound changes which were going on in Boston. The merchant who got aboard his brig or his snow for a trading venture in the Chesapeake Bay, or Charleston, or the West Indies, or to Great Britain was breaking some of the strands which bound him to his Puritan ideals and traditions. The peoples of other provinces and other lands he found quite human and in no way sold to Satan as some ministers would have him believe; he became a broader and a more enlightened man by his contact with other ideas, other cultures, other beliefs. And the wealth which he brought back made it possible for him to surround himself with beautiful things—a garden, paintings, silver—to erect a fine house and ride in a costly coach, to build up a library, perhaps to indulge in music. It was Samuel Lillie, Andrew Belcher, John Foster, Samuel Phillips, Benjamin Gallop, and others like them who led the way in transforming the capital of the Wilderness Zion into a prosperous, by no means somber, commercial town.

[2] *Boston Evening-Post,* April 19, 1742.

[3] Justin Winsor, ed., *Memorial History of Boston* (Boston: J. R. Osgood and Company, 1880–1881), II, pp. 522, 523.

The battle between the old ideas and the new as a matter of course was fought out in the schools. There were five public schools in Boston during the eighteenth century, the North Grammar School, the South Grammar School, the Queen Street Writing School, the North Writing School, and the Writing School on the Common. Tuition was free for all save the children of "strangers," parents being charged only for firewood. In 1749 there were 158 pupils in the two grammar schools and 547 in the writing schools. Since the masters and ushers received their salaries chiefly from the city authorities and were subject to frequent inspection by "learned men" who made their reports to the Selectmen, the school system reflected accurately the religious views of that body.[4] The youths who sat under John Level or Reverend Nathaniel Williams or Samuel Granger were taught to glory in the deeds of John Cotton and John Winthrop and were immunized as thoroughly as possible against the heresies of Arminius.

However, if the wealthy merchant did not consider this a good diet for his son, he had the privilege of sending him to one of several private schools. In north Boston, "near the Sign of the Red Lion," Samuel Seammell, formerly a teacher of "gentlemen volunteers" for the Navy, taught "arithmetic, geometry, algebra, fluxions, trigonometry, navigation, dialing, astronomy, surveying," etc.[5] Across the river in Cambridge, Enoch Ward kept a boarding school for instruction in Latin and Greek,[6] while Royse and Williams, in Queen Street, taught mathematics "in the lower part of the house occupied by Mr. Turner, dancing-master."[7] In 1772, Lewis Delile, who

[4] Samuel G. Drake, *The History and Antiquities of Boston* (Boston, 1857), pp. 596, 629, etc.

[5] *Boston Evening-Post*, November 28, 1737.

[6] *Ibid.*, July 18, 1748.

[7] *Ibid.*, May 24, 1762.

was educated at the University of Bordeaux, made a startling innovation by opening a school for the study of French in King Street.[8]

The Boston school teachers were well paid and seem to have been a higher type of men than some who disgraced their profession in other parts of the colonies. When Samuel Granger, after fifteen years of teaching, succumbed to apoplexy in 1734, the principal persons of the town attended his funeral, while 150 pupils preceded the casket. Reverend Nathaniel Williams, for many years master of the South Grammar School, was lauded in the press for his industry and fidelity, and his death "esteemed a public loss."[9]

The graduate from the grammar school who continued his work at Harvard found that ancient center of Puritanism seriously affected by the spirit of change. In 1724, when President John Leverett died, Cotton Mather confidently expected to be chosen in his place. It was time, he thought, to reform the college by making it once more what its founders had intended it to be, a school of the prophets, a bulwark of fundamental Calvinism. Deep was his disgust when he was passed over in favor of the learned and moderate Benjamin Wadsworth, minister of the First Church. And though his administration was marked by many student disorders, by frolics, cursings, and practical jokes, it kept the institution headed toward liberalism, both in educational policies and in freedom of thought.

Even more progressive was President Edward Holyoke, who succeeded Wadsworth and presided over the college for three decades. Harvard was still a denominational college, still upheld the tenets of Calvin, but there was enough of academic freedom to offend the conservative group and to excite the

[8] *Ibid.*, April 6, 1772.
[9] *Boston Evening-Post*, January 23, 1738.

suspicions even of the Overseers. When Whitefield came to Boston, preaching the religion of personal experience and condemning many ministers as unconverted sinners, the Harvard faculty took a strong position against him and his fellow New Lights. "It is my opinion that Dr. Tillotson is in hell for his heresy," Whitefield remarked to Henry Flynt. "It is my opinion that you will not meet him there," replied the aged Harvard tutor.

In the meanwhile the college was making advances steadily in its teaching and scholarship. Obsolete texts were replaced by Watt's *Astronomy*, Gordon's *Geographical Grammar*, Locke's *Essay Concerning Human Understanding*, and similarly stimulating books. An indication of the way things were going was the endowing of a Chair of Mathematics and Natural Philosophy by Thomas Hollis, for which the able though dissipated Isaac Greenwood was the first appointee. The students, who listened eagerly to his lectures on "the incomparable Sir Isaac Newton," were greatly disappointed at his dismissal, but they were more than compensated by the appointment of John Winthrop as his successor.

Even in student life liberal ideas were creeping in, for in 1758, despite the law forbidding acting, the students were permitted to put on productions of *Cato*, *The Recruiting Officer*, *The Orphan*, and other popular plays. They went too far, however, when in 1765 they gave a performance in which the devil was impersonated, and several were severely punished. On the whole Harvard, in this period of transition, kept its equilibrium remarkably well, not breaking with the reactionary Calvinists, but refusing to permit them to block the gradual advance toward liberalism.[10]

The conflict of the old with the new, the revolt against the

[10] Samuel E. Morison, *Three Centuries of Harvard* (Cambridge, Mass.: Harvard University Press, 1936), pp. 76–90.

mental bonds imposed by the "elect," was responsible also for much of the intellectual activity of prerevolutionary Boston. The New England ministers understood well the power of the press, and when one of them preached before the Assembly of Ministers,[11] or to the military companies on training day,[12] or after the execution of a criminal, his sermon was apt to find its way into print and to secure a wide circle of readers. If the preacher happened to touch on controversial matters or attack the Arminians or the New Lights, he would be answered in a series of pamphlets or addresses. Whitefield's quarrel with Harvard produced a deluge of charges, vindications, and counter-charges—the *Testimony* of the Harvard faculty against him, a letter calling on him to defend his conduct, another urging him to repentance, a pamphlet giving reasons for excluding him from the pulpit of a Lynn church, his vindication of his conduct and views, a defense by one of his admirers, etc.[13]

The airing of religious controversies in pamphlets and the gazettes was a comparatively new thing in Boston, since in former days the Calvinists took prompt measures to suppress any publication which dared to differ from their views. But times had changed since the day when Benjamin Franklin turned his back on the city because his brother was imprisoned for publishing in *The New England Courant* certain articles which got "under the skin" of "the great and the good." Some years later all New England was stirred by the prosecution of John Peter Zenger, publisher of the *New York Weekly Journal.* "This poor man was charged with printing . . . a libel against the governor and administration," declared an article reprinted in the *Boston Evening-Post*, "and having been

[11] *Boston Evening-Post*, September 4, 1738.
[12] *Ibid.*, July 31, 1738.
[13] *Ibid.*, January 7, 21, 28, April 8, 1745.

brought to trial, . . . he . . . was so gloriously defended by his counsel, particularly by Mr. Hamilton an old and infirm gentleman . . . that he was acquitted."[14]

Although the printing presses of mid-eighteenth century Boston indulged to the full in the new freedom won by such incidents, they by no means confined their output exclusively to religious controversies. Now and then they turned off a book of verse–*A Collection of Poems*, by Reverend John Adams, *Poems*, by members of Harvard College, etc. Much attention was given to history, and subscribers awaited eagerly the appearance of William Douglas's *British Settlements in North America*,[15] Hutchinson's *History of Massachusetts Bay*, or William Hubbard's *A Narrative of the Indian Wars in New England*. The paper-money controversy, the Stamp Act, the Boston Massacre, and other political topics came in for a large share of notice.

Strangely enough, the new Boston, with its finer houses and finer gentlemen, produced no literary work comparable to that of the reactionary group, especially Cotton Mather's *Diary* and Samuel Sewall's *Diary*. The very fact that these works were not intended for the common eye makes them the more interesting and valuable. Mather's *Diary* can hardly be called sincere, since the writer constantly tried to deceive himself, but apparently he had no intention of deceiving the public. And this very self-deception is all-revealing in its picture of a spirit which one writer, perhaps too harshly, calls "garrulous, meddlesome, scolding, an echo of dead voices," who esteemed himself, nonetheless, "a divine torch which the very hand of God had lighted."[16] Sewall, like Mather, was a

[14] *Ibid.*, May 29, 1738.

[15] *Ibid.*, November 13, 1752; June 3, 1765; April 24, 1775.

[16] Vernon L. Parrington, *The Colonial Mind* (New York: Harcourt, Brace and Company, 1927–1930), pp. 107, 108.

persistent defender of the old order, an enemy of change, but he is honest with himself and reveals the interesting combination of the hardfisted business man and religious zealot which was so characteristic of New England. The *Diary* pulses with life, brings back in vivid pictures the Boston of two centuries ago, its streets, its buildings, its people, its controversies. What Pepys was for London, Sewall was for Boston.

Since the editors of the eighteenth century, like their successors of the twentieth, catered to the public taste, we gain an insight of their reading from the pages of the *American Magazine and Historical Chronicle.* The issue for January 1746 contained articles on the proceedings of a political club, the "Difference Between Popery and Protestantism," "Drapier's Letter to the People of Ireland," "A Succinct Account of the Castle of Edinburgh," "Sir John Cape's Expedition," "Poetical Essays," "Historical Chronicle," etc.,[17] most of them reprinted from English magazines. It was a common practice, also, to reprint articles in the newspapers. The *Evening-Post,* in 1737 and 1738, published articles on "Mobs and Riots," "Spectres and Apparitions," "Of the State of Venice," "English Politicians," and "The English Constitution and the Rights of the People," taken from *The London Magazine.* Nor did it scorn to reprint matter from gazettes in other colonies, for we find articles from *The New York Gazette, The Pennsylvania Gazette,* the *Virginia Gazette,* etc.

One gains an idea of the taste of the Boston readers, also, by stepping into one of the bookshops—"The Book Store in Union Street, opposite the Corn-Field," the London Book Store, at the head of King Street, the Bible and Crown on Dock Square, or the Heart and Crown in Cornhill. Here one is sure to find Tillotson's *Works,* Plutarch's *Lives,* Locke's

[17] *Boston Evening-Post,* February 17, 1746.

Works, Wollaston's *Religion of Nature*, Rollin's *Ancient History*, the works of Milton, Pope, Hume, the various classical authors–Livy, Tacitus, Sallust, Cicero–copies of *The Tatler*, *The Rambler*, *The Spectator*, Mather's *Magnalia*, and other books on philosophy, astronomy, divinity, medicine, law, and government.[18] The contemporary novelists apparently did not enjoy in Boston the popularity which is so noticeable in the southern cities, and *Pamela*, *Clarissa*, *Peregrine Pickle*, *Roderick Random*, and *Humphrey Clinker* were rarities on the shop shelves. Possibly many who might have spent an idle hour with the novelists were frightened off by the warnings of the ministers and articles in the press. "Among all the licentious follies which corrupt the mind there is not one which has done more hurt in the present age than the vast quantity of idle and immoral books," one writer warned. "A simple amusement in reading is such a ridiculous trifling away of time that any person of common sense must on the least reflection condemn themselves."[19]

It was in 1756 that John Mein, the bookseller, started the first circulating library in Boston, with dues of £1.8 a year and with twelve hundred volumes of history, travel, biography, drama, fiction, divinity, medicine, science, poetry, husbandry, navigation, law, etc. "Something of this kind has been long wanted," stated Mein, "to amuse the man of leisure, to afford an elegant and agreeable relaxation to the minds of men of business and to insinuate knowledge and instruction under the veil of entertainment to the fair sex. Here likeways the Divine and the Christian may find in the works of the pious and the learned that exalted satisfaction which flows from the serious study of the Christian religion; the merchant may meet

[18] *Ibid.*, April 3, 1738; June 8, 1767; March 9, 1767, etc.
[19] *Ibid.*, April 3, 1738.

with a complete history and description of those countries to which he has traded."[20]

The Puritan scholar wandered unsuspectingly into the field of science. Since there could be no conflict between revealed and physical truth, scientific discoveries could only buttress the Christian faith as interpreted by Calvin. It is true that Sewall was a bit nervous when Cotton Mather committed himself in a sermon to the Copernican system and jotted down in his *Diary*, "I think it inconvenient to assert such problems."[21] But both in England and in the colonies the Calvinist colleges took the lead in the study of mathematics, astronomy, physics, and geography, and Puritan divines and other leading churchmen interested themselves in zoölogy, biology, and other sciences.

It is this which explains why Cotton Mather, who was an ardent believer in all kinds of supernatural occurrences and wrote a book in support of the reality of witches, could be a member of the Royal Society, an enthusiastic scientist, and a supporter of advanced practice in medicine. He collected and sent to England in 1714 specimens of bones, fossil teeth, and other curiosities; his notes on the moose, rattlesnake, pigeon, and fishes reveal him as a keen observer of New England fauna, while his treatment for yellow fever and his records of snow, wind, rain, thunder, and lightning attest the breadth of his scientific interests.

Paul Dudley, of Roxbury, won distinction not only as a horticulturist, but because of his studies of New England animals and his observations of earthquakes. His "Essay upon the Natural History of Whales," published by the Royal Society, attracted especial interest, while he became an authority upon

[20] *Ibid.*, November 18, 1765.

[21] Samuel Sewall, *Diary* (Boston, 1878–1882), II, p. 31.

the habits of the moose, deer, and snakes, partly by personal observation, partly through conversations with Indians. Zabdiel Boylston deserves undying honor as the first physician to practise inoculation for smallpox in the colonies and the widest and most successful inoculator of his time. With public sentiment against him, in the face of threatened prosecution, he continued on his course, heartened however by the support of Cotton Mather, until he had fully demonstrated the value of this method of combating the dreaded disease. Equally praiseworthy was John Winthrop, collector and student of minerals, fossils, shells, and a leader in establishing mineralogy as a science.[22]

Though the old Puritan group entered fully into the literary and scientific life of the colony, it was the wealthy merchants and officials who were chiefly responsible for the flowering of the arts—the development of architecture, painting, the artistic crafts. The Puritans brought with them from East Anglia a distinct and pleasing domestic architecture, characterized by half-timber construction, the overhang, dew drop, and the multiple gable. No doubt, the first houses at Boston were as nearly replicas of the yeoman cottage of Essex or Suffolk as wilderness conditions permitted. But the severe New England winters, the lack of lime, the abundance of wood, the dearness of labor soon effected a change, so that a distinctive Massachusetts architecture began to emerge. The quaint old Fairbanks house, Dedham, with its great expanse of back roof; the House of the Seven Gables; the Paul Revere house, Boston; the John Ward house, Salem; and many others attest the individuality as well as beauty of the seventeenth-century Puritan residence.

[22] Frederick E. Brasch, *The Royal Society, etc.* (privately printed, 1931), pp. 13–21.

But the new aristocracy, with its close tie with England, broke with the local architectural traditions, just as it rebelled against the old Puritan restrictions upon personal conduct. The fine residences which began to rear their heads on Purchase Street or Garden Court Street or Beacon Street were taken out of English books of architecture, so that Boston became more and more a Georgian town in outward appearance. Many relics of the earlier era remained—shops with their multipaned windows, quaint old tenement houses, their upper stories projecting over the streets—but the pride of the town were the James Bowdoin house, the Gardiner Greene place, the Edward Bromfield house, and other Georgian mansions.

Gone was the overhang and dew drop, gone the casement windows, gone the central chimney, to make room for the balanced facade with the same number of windows on either side of the classic doorway, the roof pierced by dormers and perhaps surmounted by a balustrade. One entered a wide hallway flanked by two rooms on either side, between which rose the chimneys. Unfortunately these old houses have disappeared, but their memory long lingered with the older generation of Bostonians who never wearied of dwelling upon the glories of the Hutchinson house or the Andrews house. And we are left in no doubt of their appearance, not only because many descriptions have come down to us, but since they were similar in design and appearance to many surviving Georgian houses at Cambridge, Salem, and elsewhere.

Typical was the Frankland house on Garden Court Street. "It was built of brick, three stories high and contained in all twenty-six rooms. A spacious hall ran through the center from which arose a flight of stairs. . . . The parlors were ornamented with fluted columns elaborately carved, and richly gilded pilasters and cornices; the walls were wainscoted and the panels embellished with beautiful landscape scenery; the mantelpieces were of Italian marble and the fireplaces of the finest porcelain. . . . The floor of the eastern parlor was laid in diamond-shaped figures and had in the center a tessellated design . . . in mahogany, ebony, satin-wood, etc. encircling the coat-of-arms of the Clarke family."[23]

Equally noted was the residence of Governor Thomas Hutchinson, which was sacked and partly burned by a mob in August 1765, in protest against the Stamp Act and the Sugar Act and as an expression of hatred of the British ruling class. The house was of brick, in the Georgian style, the façade ornamented with pilasters and with a representation of the British crown over every window. "The hall of entrance displayed a spacious arch, from the roof of which a dimly lighted lamp gave a rich twilight view. The finely carved and gilded arch in massy magnificence was ornamented with busts and statues. The light streamed full on the soul-beaming countenance of Cicero . . . the panelling of the parlor was of the dark, richly shaded mahogany of St. Domingo and elaborately ornamented. . . . The library was hung with canvas-tapestry emblazoning the coronation of George III."[24]

That the congregations were not immune from the new architectural ideas is shown by the discarding of the old-type meetinghouses for real churches with steeples, built in the style of Sir Christopher Wren. Old South, built in 1729, with its arched multipaned windows, its square tower, supporting an octagonal arched superstructure capped by a graceful spire, ushered in a new epoch in New England church architecture. In every part of Massachusetts, in Connecticut, even in New Jersey, the old four-square meetinghouses with the

[23] *Memorial History of Boston*, II, p. 451.
[24] *Ibid.*, p. 527.

roof rising on four sides to the belfry gave way to more graceful structures in the style of Old South. The New England Renaissance churches, built of wood most of them, could not duplicate the classical ornamentation so notable in St. Mary-le-Bow and other Wren churches, but what they lacked in ornateness they made up in simplicity and correctness of proportion.

The wealthy Bostonian turned to the local store for engravings by famous artists and portraits of distinguished persons with which to decorate the walls of his residence. The London Book-Store advertised in 1762 that it had just imported "a very great collection of pictures, containing all the celebrated and reigning beauties in Britain, all the statesmen, generals and admirals that have distinguished themselves in this war, framed and gilded in the most elegant and neat manner. Also large and splendid views of some of the most remarkable places in North America, and of the most magnificent palaces and gardens in England."[25] William Price, at the old glass and picture shop in Cornhill, had for sale "a great variety of fine prints and prospects . . . fine large and small metzotinto prints, frames and glasses, etc."[26]

Not all the pictures came from abroad, for there were engravers in Boston who did very creditable work. Nathaniel Hurd, the silversmith, advertised that he had made "striking likenesses of his Majesty King George III, Mr. Pitt and General Wolfe, fit for a picture or for gentlemen and ladies to put in their watches."[27] Paul Revere, despite his many other activities, found time to engrave pictures of *Harvard College*, *The Repeal of the Stamp Act*, *A View of Boston Harbor*, *The*

[25] *Boston Evening-Post*, May 10, 1762.
[26] *Ibid.*, June 3, 1754.
[27] *Ibid.*, November 22, 1762.

Landing of the British in 1774, etc. The most famous of his prints is *The Boston Massacre*, showing the British soldiers firing on the mob, with the old State House in the background. Preceding Revere by many years was Peter Pelham, who had earned a reputation before coming to America about 1725 as a competent mezzotint scraper. In 1750 he painted the portraits of four Boston Episcopal ministers and gave notice to gentlemen who wished to subscribe to the engravings that he would sell them for one dollar a set.[28]

The chief importance of Pelham was the inspiration and encouragement he gave to his stepson, the youthful John Singleton Copley. This strange genius, reared in his mother's tobacco shop in Boston, uneducated, self-taught in his art, who never saw a really good painting until he was fully grown, was the greatest of American colonial painters. Benjamin West acquired distinction by going to Europe and is rightly considered more English than American; Copley's best work was done before he left American soil. His greatness lay in his ability to catch soul-revealing expressions in the faces of his subjects.

Copley sent his *Boy with the Squirrel* to England where it received great praise and West wrote urging him to come to Europe for study and inspiration. His timidity kept him at home for several years, during which time he produced some of his best pictures, and when, at last, on the eve of the Revolution, he set sail for England never to return, he bade goodbye not only to his native land but to all that was best in his art. In London he enjoyed a season of great popularity, his *Death of Chatham* winning wide applause, but thereafter his work steadily deteriorated. In seeking to imitate the European

[28] *Ibid.*, October 1, 1750; James T. Flexner, *America's Old Masters* (New York: Viking Press, 1939), pp. 108, 109.

artists Copley lost the realism, the power to reveal character which had marked his work in America, without acquiring the grace of a Reynolds or a Gainsborough.

The Bostonian might have his mansion filled with fine furniture and silverware, with perhaps a Copley portrait on his wall, but he was not permitted to attend the theater. "The government being in the hands of dissenters they don't admit of plays," Bennett wrote in 1740. It was in 1714 that the new spirit of gaiety first ran afoul of the old puritanical spirit. "There is a rumor as if some designed to have a play acted in the Council chamber next Monday, which surprises me," wrote Samuel Sewall. "And as much as in me lies, I do forbid it. The Romans were very fond of their plays, but I never heard they were so far set upon them as to turn their Senate house into a play house. . . . Let not Christian Boston go beyond heathen Rome in the practice of shameful vanities."[29]

This seems to have put a quietus upon the theater until 1750, when a group of amateurs, assisted by two English professionals, presented Thomas Otway's tragedy, *The Orphan*, in a State Street coffee house. This was such a novelty that a crowd assembled far greater than the room would accommodate, and a near riot was the result. Thereupon the General Court passed a law forbidding acting and rendering both players and spectators liable to fine.[30] However, in 1767 it was notorious that private plays and tragedies were presented with impunity. "I well remember a few years since, when a number of young gentlemen entertained some of their friends with a noble and decent comedy or tragedy, a method was soon found to stop them," declared a correspondent in the *Evening-Post*. "With

[29] *Memorial History of Boston*, II, p. 6.

[30] Arthur Hornblow, *A History of the Theatre in America* (Philadelphia: J. B. Lippincott, 1919), I, pp. 33, 34.

more propriety should those of so insignificant a character be prevented. . . . It is apprehended that when the American Company of Comedians . . . hear there is so great an inclination for such entertainments in this place they will endeavor to introduce themselves and certainly with more justice than these bunglars."[31] This fear proved groundless, and it was only with the Revolution, when the British officers put on *The Blockade of Boston*, that the old blue laws at last broke down.

Though the colonial Bostonian could not indulge in the theater, in time he insisted upon and made good his right to hear fine music. In 1773 the prejudice against public concerts had so nearly gone that the Selectmen gave their assent to a performance in Faneuil Hall, under the direction of W. S. Morgan. The concert opened with an overture and continued with a song, an overture from the *Shepherd's Lottery*, a song, a harpsichord concerto, chorus from *The Messiah*, the *Coronation Anthem*, a violin solo, an overture, and concluded with a liberty song. There were "upwards of fifty performers."[32] That the hatred for the British garrison two years before the outbreak of the Revolution was not shared by all classes of Bostonians is shown by the participation of the band of the Sixty-fourth Regiment in a performance at the Concert Hall, in which Handel's overtures alternated with violin solos, vocal duets, an organ concerto, etc.[33]

Morgan, who advertised himself as a "pupil of Signor Giardini," played on the organ, violin, and harpsichord, was a composer of songs and symphonies, and gave instruction in music to ladies and gentlemen. Equally versatile was William Selby, organist and composer, who arrived from London

[31] *Boston Evening-Post*, April 6, 1767.
[32] *Ibid.*, October 25, 1773.
[33] *Ibid.*, September 10, 1773.

about 1771. In his initial appearance he played his own *Concerto on the Organ* and his *Harpsichord Concerto*. His interest in choral music made him the forerunner of the Handel and Haydn Society. Other important figures in the musical life of colonial Boston were Josiah Flagg, a compiler of psalm tunes and a promoter of concert music; one Steiglitz, "a capital performer on the German flute"; and David Propert, organist of Trinity Church and concert master.[34]

In church music the Puritans for a century deviated not at all from the metrical psalmody, familiar to all in Old Hundred and published in the Bay Psalm Book. Since the early books gave only the words and not the music, it became customary for an elder or precentor to line out the psalm, or sing a line and then pause while the congregation repeated it. Early in the eighteenth century when the psalm books were printed with music as well as the words, a bitter battle had to be waged before this absurd custom was abandoned. Even then, the use of instruments, even of organs, to add to the beauty of the music, had to be deferred to later decades. In the last years of the colonial period occurred a still greater break with custom, when William Billings produced *The New England Psalm Singer*, with its so-called "fuging pieces." This was an important declaration of independence and though his meaningless repetitions added little to the charm of church music, they led the way for the hymnology of Lowell Mason, Thomas Hastings, and other early nineteenth-century composers.

From a very early period the artistic spirit in Boston found an outlet in the creation of fine silverware. The Puritan ideals which were so suspicious of secular music and scorned painting as trivial were not opposed to the shaping of graceful

[34] J. T. Howard, *Our American Music* (New York: Thomas Y. Crowell, 1931), pp. 62, 69.

beakers, tankards, porringers, and teapots. Fortunately the simplicity which was demanded added to rather than detracted from the charm of the early pieces. In both church and domestic silverware the Boston craftsmen—John Hull, Robert Sanderson, Jeremiah Drummer, Timothy Dwight, John Coney, Edward Winslow, and others—were masters, leaders in the colonial field. The beauty of their work shows partly in the form, which is always simple, always graceful; partly in the decoration, which is never overornate; and partly in the texture and color of the surface.[35]

With the increase of wealth in the mid-eighteenth century the demand for fine silver increased steadily and a new generation of craftsmen continued the output of tankards, teapots, coffeepots, porringers, etc. Yielding in outward form to the changing styles in England, these men held out firmly against the overornamentation so characteristic of the English rococo, with its riot of flowers, leaves, shells, and scrolls. The outstanding change was the bellying out into the inverted pear shape of teapots, coffeepots, sugar bowls, and cream jugs. Notable among the silversmiths of this period were Samuel Edwards, the three Burts—Benjamin, Samuel, and William—John Coburn, Samuel Minott, and Paul Revere. The fame of the last named as a courier in the Revolution has overshadowed his career as an artistic craftsman, yet he ranks high among early American silversmiths. The exhibit of Revere silver at the Boston Museum of Fine Arts in 1906 revealed the worth of his teapots, porringers, sugar bowls, mugs, tankards, and other pieces, both in beauty of design and in workmanship. Revere lived to be eighty-three years old, so that his career extended well into the period of the classic revival, but his talent was

[35] C. L. Avery, *Early American Silver* (New York: The Century Company, 1930), pp. xix, xlvii–li.

equal to the change, and his later creamers, sugar bowls, and teapots with their fluted sides and pendent festoons surpass in delicacy and beauty the best of his earlier pieces.[36]

It is surprising that the silversmiths should have been able to hold their own in the face of English competition. That this competition was keenly felt we gather from a notice by Daniel Henchman in the *Boston Evening-Post* in which he asked the public to give him the preference over "those strangers among us who import and sell English plate, to the great hurt and prejudice of the townsmen who have been bred in the business."[37] One wonders why Boston produced no group of cabinetmakers comparable to her fine silversmiths. The weight and bulk of tables, chairs, and secretaries, with the consequent high freight rates, must have constituted at least some protection to the local craftsmen against English competition, whereas the cost of transporting silver must have been slight.

As we review the cultural life of Boston in the eighteenth century it is the intellectual activity which stands out, and presents such a great contrast with the intellectual life of the South. William Byrd took his Latin, Greek, and Hebrew authors, or the sermons of the good parish minister, very much as he would take a bottle of wine, as something already prepared for the good of his mind and soul. But the Bostonians wanted to have a hand themselves in the fermenting of their intellectual wine, and though what they produced was often a bit sour, at least it was in part their own creation. When Whitefield visited Virginia to deliver his thundering sermons and threaten the people with damnation, there were some who regarded him as a prophet, others condemned him as a fanatic,

[36] *Ibid.*, pp. 99–102, 145–149.

[37] January 4, 1773.

but neither side rushed into print with letters to the gazettes and volley after volley of pamphlets as they did in Boston.

In artistic matters the achievements of the Bostonians were remarkable when one considers that they were living in a provincial town, torn as it were between its cultural dependence upon England and its loyalty to the traditions of its Puritan founders. On the eve of the Revolution the place could boast of a polite society, interested not only in trade, politics, and religion, but in architecture, literature, music, and fine silverware. Though the wealthy families looked down upon their one really talented artist as a mere craftsman whose sole task was to produce accurate likenesses, they were beginning to show some real appreciation of art for art's sake. If we are to understand the Boston of the nineteenth century with its keen interest in American literature, in music, art, and architecture, we must know the Boston of colonial days, the Boston of Samuel Sewall, Cotton Mather, Peter Faneuil, John Hancock, Thomas Hutchinson, Paul Revere, and John Singleton Copley.

FATHER KNICKERBOCKER BECOMES AESTHETIC

New York

NEW YORK in the eighteenth century was a Dutch town slowly changing into a provincial English city. In the little schoolrooms on Maiden Lane or Beaver Street, in the Calvinist churches, in the shops of the silversmiths and the cabinet-makers, in the offices of the architects and carpenters the battle was waged between Dutch civilization and English civilization. The man who wrote in 1718 that a lot had been granted to Barent Van Kleeck for the "behoof of the Inhabitance and Naborhod of pochkepsen aforesaid to Bild and Maentaen a proper Mietinghouse to worship" unconsciously revealed the changes which were going on,[1] changes not only from the Dutch to the English tongue, but from Dutch to English customs, literature, architecture, education.

Yet the process was slow, at times almost imperceptible. The traveler Burnaby tells us that as late as 1760 more than half of the people, and almost all the merchants, were Dutch. Had we strolled along Maiden Lane or lower Nassau Street at this time, we would have walked between rows of Dutch houses, all with the gable ends toward the street; had we entered one of the bookshops, we would have discovered that

[1] Irving Elting, *Dutch Village Communities on the Hudson River*, Johns Hopkins Studies (Baltimore: Johns Hopkins Press, 1886), IV, p. 40.

Dutch influence

many of the schoolbooks, psalmbooks, and other volumes displayed for sale were in Dutch; had we inquired the price, we would have received an answer in Dutch or in English thickly flavored with Dutch. After the Battle of Long Island, when the Americans set fire to New York to keep it from serving as a base for the British, it was largely a Dutch town which went up in smoke.

Involved in the clash of these two Old World civilizations, and yet separate from it, was the gradual development of an American culture. When the Dutch Reformed Church slowly, almost unwillingly, broke the bonds which tied it to the classis of Amsterdam, it became an independent American organization, with its own educational system and its own governing body. It was the Georgian architecture taken from the books of English designers which superseded the medieval and the Renaissance buildings of lower Manhattan, yet a Georgian tinctured with American ideas, built of American materials to suit American needs. New York was no more ready than Boston or Philadelphia to declare cultural independence prior to or even after the Revolution, but the process of Americanization was well under way, even in the days of Governor Hunter or Governor William Burnet.

Nothing better than the famous Zenger trial shows the growth of the American spirit, which in its essence was the spirit of freedom. When William Cosby came over as governor in 1732, he immediately assumed such arbitrary powers as to arouse the bitter opposition of all save a small court party. He refused to hold a new election, bullied his council into obedience, snubbed all who opposed his slightest whim. Against this tyranny John Peter Zenger launched a bitter attack in the pages of his *New York Weekly Journal.* One of the governor's friends was represented first as a mon-

significance of Zenger trial?

key, then as a spaniel; Cosby himself was lampooned; the court dinners were denounced as wasteful and corrupt. When Zenger was warned that respect was due the governor's position, his paper retorted: "If all governors are to be reverenced, why not the Turk and old Muley or Nero?"

Cosby struck back by burning certain copies of the *Journal* "near the pillory by the hands of the common hangman," and indicting Zenger for libel. When two able advocates came forward to defend him, the Governor expelled them from the New York Bar. It seemed that there would be no one to take their place until the day of trial, when the distinguished attorney, Andrew Hamilton, of Philadelphia, then old and infirm, arose to plead the case. In eloquent words he defended the liberty of the press. "Shall not the oppressed have even the right to complain, shall the press be silenced that evil governors may have their way? . . . Old and weak as I am, I should think it my duty if required to go to the utmost part of the land where my services could be of use in assisting to quench the flame of prosecutions set on foot by the government to deprive a people of the right of remonstrating. . . . The question before the court . . . is not the cause of a poor printer, nor of New York alone, . . . [but] of every free man that lives under a British government on the main of America." When the verdict of "not guilty" was announced, the crowd which leaped to their feet cheering wildly were not Dutchmen, were not English; they were Americans.

Yet the new culture, which found its chief advocates in the wealthy group of merchants surrounding the governor and seeking his favors, was patterned after the culture of Georgian England. The houses which reared their heads in the district north of Wall Street were usually built on the Georgian model; furniture in the Chippendale style made its way into the reception rooms; the silversmiths gave their tankards and beakers an English flavor; English books multiplied in libraries and bookshops; troops of English actors appeared to present *Othello* or *Romeo and Juliet* at the Nassau Street Theatre.

In the days of Peter Stuyvesant the children of New Amsterdam went of course to Dutch schools, taught by Dutchmen—Adam Roelantsen, Jan Stevensen, William Vestensz, and others. Although the schools were the joint concern of church and state and the masters drilled their young charges in the catechism, some of them were by no means models of piety and good conduct. The school was kept in the largest room of the master's residence, and here, at eight in the morning at the sound of the horn, the children assembled, the boys raising their caps to the teacher as they sought their seats. Then began the day's recitations from the alphabet book, selections from Old and New Testaments, perhaps the history of David, followed by the singing of a psalm and a concluding prayer. The rules of conduct were posted for all to see and a minor infringement brought a slap on the hand with the *plak*, a more serious offense a few blows with the dreaded *roede*.[2]

With the English conquest the Dutch schools found their two sources of support, the Reformed Church and the town government, no longer working in harmony. The Church wished ardently to perpetuate the Dutch language, while the municipality leaned more and more to English. Although Dutch parents and the domines insisted that children should attend the Dutch schools, the drift to English schools became more and more pronounced, since the young people became ashamed of their inability to speak good English and insisted upon instruction in the prevailing tongue. By the middle of

[2] W. H. Kilpatrick, *The Dutch Schools of New Netherland* (Washington, D. C.: Government Printing Office, 1912), p. 226.

the eighteenth century we find Augustus Vaughan conducting an English school in New Street near Beaver;[3] B. Leigh and Garrat Noel on Broad Street near the long bridge;[4] Charles Johnston on Hanover Square; while Latin schools which prepared boys for college were opened by Robert Leeth, on Wall Street, Alexander Miller near Hanover Square, and by others.[5] That teaching in Dutch was continued at this time, however, we know from a notice in the *Gazette* inserted by Reinhold Jan Klockhoff that he gave courses in Dutch, French, Latin, arithmetic, and geography at the residence of John Peter Zenger's widow, on Golden Hill.[6]

Had one visited the English school of John Lewis, which seems to have been typical, one would have found the good master instructing the pupils in "speaking, reading, spelling and writing English"; explaining arithmetic, vulgar and decimal fractions, and extracting the square and cube roots; revealing the mysteries of navigation, geometry, and trigonometry; touching upon the "elements of geography and astronomy, with several other useful branches of the mathematics and literature." The school was limited to thirty scholars and tuition was higher than in other New York schools. Nonetheless, Lewis had to earn additional income by drawing up and engrossing bonds, bills, deeds, etc., "at reasonable rates."[7]

It was in January 1747 that the *New York Gazette* announced the issuing of 10,000 lottery tickets, the profits from which were to be used for the founding of King's College. "As such a laudable design will greatly tend to the welfare and reputation of this colony, it is expected the inhabitants

[3] *New York Gazette*, October 5, 1747.
[4] *Ibid.*, December 31, 1750.
[5] *Ibid.*, December 24, 1764.
[6] *Ibid.*, April 1, 1751.
[7] *Ibid.*, June 11, 1753.

will readily be excited to be adventurers."[8] That many did become excited is evident from the statement that by January 1752 no less than £3,443 had been raised. So the trustees erected a building in the suburbs, where today Murray and Barclay Streets meet Church Street, on the general plan of Nassau Hall at Princeton, elected Reverend Samuel Johnson president, and began instruction in 1754. Although avowedly nondenominational, the college was controlled by the Anglicans.

A very small fraction indeed of the thousands of young people who today crowd the classes of Columbia University could have gained admission to the infant King's College, for the first requisite was the ability to write "a good legible hand," and another the "construing and passing" of two or three of the orations of Tully and the first books of *The Aeneid* and some of the chapters of the Gospel of St. John in Greek.[9] The college sought to steer the students into "a serious, virtuous and industrious course of life," while instructing them in "the learned languages and in the arts of reasoning exactly, writing correctly and speaking eloquently, and in the arts of numbering and measuring, of surveying and navigation, of geography and history, of husbandry, commerce and government; and in the knowledge of all nature in the heavens above us and in the air, water and earth around us, and of the various kinds of meteors, stones, mines and minerals, plants and animals."[10] A large order this, doing credit to President Johnson and the trustees, and setting a standard for the little college which augured well for the future.

One group of Dutch had favored the founding of King's

[8] *Ibid.*, January 12, 1747.
[9] *Ibid.*, June 17, 1754.
[10] *Ibid.*

College in the expectation that it would include a theological professorship to train ministers for the Reformed Church. But others saw in it nothing more than a scheme to draw off Dutch youth from their allegiance to their church, language, and traditions. "We must unite with the members of the Church of England in promoting their high church college," wrote one Dutchman sarcastically, "in order to get our youth so freely educated that they forever renounce their own Church, and when they get into the Assembly make us pay for it. . . . Is this a basis whereon to fix a seminary of learning in a free land, designed for a place of refuge . . . in which the encroaching party is perhaps scarcely a twentieth man at present?"[11]

Perhaps it was not by chance that the founding of the first New York public library took place the same year that King's College opened its doors. One evening in 1754, William Smith, one of the founders of Princeton College, Philip Livingston, William Alexander, William Livingston, and others met to launch the Society Library for the promotion of "a spirit of inquiry among the people." It was hoped that a royal charter would be granted and that a building could be erected not only to house the books, but a museum and observatory as well.[12] In 1763, Garrat Noel, the bookseller, opened a rival library, "consisting of several thousand volumes," next door to the Merchants Coffee House. "All persons that choose to spend their leisure hours in reading may be supplied from this source of laudable amusement a whole year at the easy rate of four dollars," he announced in the *Gazette*.

We may assume that there were very few Dutch books in either of these libraries, but that Dutch families could procure

[11] Thomas E. V. Smith, *The City of New York* (1789), pp. 190, 191.
[12] James G. Wilson, ed., *Memorial History of the City of New York* (New York: New York History Company, 1892–1893), II, pp. 303, 304.

Nation's greatest public library

volumes in their native tongue we learn from the advertisement of James Aarding, near the Meat Market, and other booksellers. Among Aarding's offerings were *Bruyns Reizen*, *Holmes Woordenbook*, *Beginsehn Van Euclides*, *Werdadize Meethoust*, etc.[13] But at Hugh Gaine's shop, at the New Printing Office in Beaver Street, at Noel's store in Broad Street, and elsewhere the stock was overwhelmingly English. The dealers seem to have played no favorites, for on their shelves Philip Doddridge's books rubbed elbows with those of Archbishop Tillotson, *Pilgrim's Progress* with the *Westminster Confession of Faith*, Voltaire with Watt's *Rational Foundation of the Christian Church*. As in other colonial cities, reading in New York was not only becoming general, but embraced a wide field of interest. A casual inspection of the stock at the New Printing Office reveals volumes on religion, the classics, medicine, philosophy, travel, history, surveying, fiction, government, etc.[14]

Not only were there no Dutch circulating libraries, but very few private Dutch libraries comparable to those of the well-to-do English families. The average Dutchman had only his massive Bible, adorned with heavy silver clasps, which had come down to him from his ancestors, the Dutch almanacs, and perhaps a few other volumes. The domine alone, who was a university graduate and a man of learning, gathered together enough books to constitute a real library. Domine Rensselaer's library of two hundred volumes, embracing works in several languages, was no doubt typical.[15]

Since the Dutch were not habitual readers, they were handicapped in the struggle of languages by the meager output of

[13] *New York Gazette*, May 11, 1747.
[14] *Ibid.*, September 23, 1751.
[15] *Drie Predicatien*, 1721.

their presses. There were no newspapers in Dutch, no magazines, and a mere handful of books and pamphlets on religious topics and a few on politics or education. Only in the heated controversy between the American and the Dutch factions in the Church were the Dutch presses kept busy, airing the views of both sides in pamphlets and printed sermons—Frelinghuysen's sermons on *The Broken Heart*, *The Lord's Supper*, and *Christian Discipline; A Complaint Against Theodorus Jacobus Frelinghuysen*, etc.[16] Some of George Whitefield's sermons were printed in Dutch by Zenger, while others by Jonathan Edwards were struck off in the shop in "den Nieuw Druckery in de Bever-Straat."

Even among the English, the atmosphere of the colony was mercantile and materialistic, rather than intellectual. "Tho' the province of New York abounds certainly more in riches than any other of the northern colonies, yet there has been less care to propagate knowledge or learning," complained Cadwallader Colden in 1748. "The only principle of life propagated among the young people is to get money, and men are only esteemed according to what they are worth—that is, the money they are possessed of."[17] Yet New York was by no means indifferent to the intellectual and cultural awakening which was affecting colonial thinking and living so profoundly in the second half of the eighteenth century. Of this the founding of King's College was proof enough, but it found expression also in an increasing interest in scientific discoveries—in electricity, botany, zoölogy, chemistry, etc.

Colden's own career was a refutation of his charge, for he

[16] *Klagte Van Eenige Leeden der Nederduytse Hervormde Kerk* (New York: J. P. Zenger, 1725), etc.

[17] Esther Singleton, *Social New York under the Georges* (New York: D. Appleton and Company, 1902), pp. 314, 315.

won distinction as botanist, philosopher, mathematician, and medical scientist. A successful doctor, merchant, and government official, for years the acting governor of New York, busy drawing up an Indian policy for the colony, and protecting the royal lands from greedy monopolists, he found time to devote to scientific investigation and writing. Linnaeus, Gronovius, Franklin, Collinson, and Samuel Johnson corresponded with him, admired his work, and encouraged him to give his conclusions to the public. Among his best known productions in the field of physics are *The Principle of Action in Matter*, *Light and Colors*, *The Cohesion of the Parts of Bodies;* in medicine *An Account of the Climate and Diseases of New York*, *Observations on the Yellow Fever in Virginia*, and two papers on the treatment of cancer; in philosophy *The First Principles of Morality or the Actions of Intelligent Beings* and *An Introduction to the Study of Philosophy*.

The changing New York, with its dying Dutch civilization and its budding English culture, may be studied to better advantage in architecture than in any other medium. In the days of Peter Minuit and Peter Stuyvesant the town was as Dutch in its architecture as though it were located on the Zuider Zee rather than the Hudson. Although time has been unkind to New Amsterdam, so that scarcely a vestige of it remains amid the skyscrapers of lower Manhattan, we can follow the changes that took place through the unusually large number of views which have come down to us and have been made available to the student in the pages of I. N. Phelps Stokes's remarkable *Iconography of New York*.

The first settlers on Manhattan seem to have built of wood, and in the Prototype View of 1650 we see a succession of little frame houses stretching along the shore, whose steep roof lines, curved gables, and vertical boarding remind us of Alkmaar or Edam. In time, however, stone and brick houses raised their heads on the Strand or on Broad Street, with the stepped, or the Flemish, or the concave gables so typical of the mother country. In the Dutch cities, where frontage on the streets and canals was very costly, the houses were long and narrow, with the entrance through the gable end, and in New Amsterdam, although the need no longer existed, the custom was adhered to. Since the gable end was the only part of the structure visible to the public, upon it the builders lavished their decorations—the finial, the beam anchor, the recessed windows, colored brickwork, glazed tiles. Even the roofs of New Amsterdam expressed the Dutch spirit, for their red and black pantiles, contrasting strangely with the green background of the New Jersey woods, were strikingly suggestive of Delft or Groningen or Hoorn.

With the English conquest, the aspect of the town began to change, as Georgian architecture succeeded the medieval Dutch. The Dutch in this, as in other matters, resisted stubbornly, and the fact that a Burnet or a Cosby sat in the governor's seat did not prevent them from continuing to build in the traditional style. Yet year after year, decade after decade, English architecture gained ground. As one stood on the riverbank looking over the East River at the massed houses of the town, one saw, even in the section below Wall Street, here and there a house built in the English style, while further north Dutch architecture became the exception rather than the rule. And when, in 1776, the great fire wiped out street after street of quaint old Dutch houses, they were replaced in large measure by buildings in the English style.

The Abraham de Peyster house, on Pearl Street, furnishes a striking illustration of the transition from Dutch to Georgian architecture, for it was a medley of the two styles. The front façade, with its classic front door surmounted by a balcony, its ornate central Palladian window, its flat arches, shows clearly the influence of Gibbs or Halfpenny; but the tiled gambrel roof, with its elongated dormers, takes us back to the days when the town was still New Amsterdam.[18] Before the midcentury mark had been reached, however, the architects were making a point of emphasizing their training in the Georgian school, and the house which showed a trace of Dutch influence was quite outmoded. In 1765, Dobie and Clow, in Division Street, stated in *The New York Mercury* that they were prepared to build "after the London taste."[19] Three years later Willoughby Loftus "informed the public" that he had "acquired the art of forming designs for buildings" and that gentlemen who favored him with their patronage could depend on having their work done "in the newest and neatest manner now practiced in or about London."[20]

Typical of the new style, and famous in its day, was the residence of the wealthy merchant, William Walton, which stood where Pearl Street now touches Franklin Square, facing west, but looking out over green fields in the rear to the East River. It is described as "a brick edifice, fifty feet in front and three stories high, built with Holland bricks relieved by brown stone water-tables, lentils and jams, with walls as substantial as many modern churches." The staircase in the great hall, with mahogany handrails and bannisters, "would not have disgraced a nobleman's palace,"[21] while the classic door with its Corinthian columns and broken pediment, the ballustraded roof covered with tiles, the flat arches of the windows, the

[18] Compare the Samuel Kip house, built in 1641.

[19] April 8, 1765.

[20] *New York Gazette*, June 27, 1768.

[21] *New York Mirror*, March 17, 1832.

quoins, the costly paneling of the interior gave an impression of luxury and grandeur.[22]

In New York, as elsewhere, the Calvinist groups strongly condemned the theater and denounced all actors as depraved wretches bent on corrupting society and misleading the young. But these groups were not strong enough to keep them out of the city, so that New York audiences were enjoying productions of Shakespeare and other writers for decades before they were tolerated in Boston. It was in 1732 that a band of English professionals arrived in the city, and leasing a large room in a building belonging to Rip Van Dam, near the junction of Pearl Street and Maiden Lane, opened on December 6 with *The Recruiting Officer*. That they were assisted by local talent is shown by the fact that the part of Worthy was acted by the "ingenious Mr. Hardy, barber and peruke-maker to his Honor."[23] The company continued to give regular performances until February 1734 when they disbanded.

It is difficult to locate the early New York theaters, since they seem to have been moved at intervals from the storeroom of one old Dutch building to another. These rooms were on the second floor, and, as it was customary to bring in bales and boxes through a door opening above the street by means of a block and tackle, the stairs must have been steep and narrow and the means of exit in case of fire very inadequate. The plan of New York in 1735 shows a "play house" on Broadway near the Battery, but the very next year we hear of the new theater on Dock Street. T. Allston Brown, in *A History of the New York Stage*, thus describes one of these early makeshift playhouses. "The stage was raised five feet from the floor. The scenes, curtains and wings were all carried by the managers in

[22] *Memorial History of the City of New York*, II, p. 306.
[23] *New England and Boston Gazette*, December 11, 1732.

their property trunks. A green curtain was suspended from the ceiling. A pair of paper screens were erected upon the right and left hand sides for wings. Six wax lights were in front of the stage. The orchestra consisted of a German flute, horn and drum players. Suspended from the ceiling was the chandelier, made of a barrel hoop, through which were driven half a dozen nails into which were stuck so many candles. Two drop scenes representing a castle and a wood, bits of landscape river and mountain comprised the scenery."[24]

As late as 1750 this type of warehouse theater seems to have been the best that New York could offer. "Last week arrived here a company of comedians from Philadelphia," announced the *Postboy* in February of that year, "who we hear have taken a convenient room for their purpose in one of the buildings belonging to the Honorable Rip Van Dam, Esq., deceased, in Nassau Street." Here, two weeks later, having gained the permission of Governor George Clinton, they presented "Richard III, wrote originally by Shakespeare and altered by Colly Cibber, Esq.," with Thomas Kean in the role of the hunchback king. Then followed *The Orphan*, Farquhar's *Sir Harry Wildair*, *The Beaux' Stratagem*, *The Beggar's Opera*, *A Bold Stroke for a Wife*, *The Mock Doctor*, *Damon and Phillida*, *Miss in Her Teens*, and other favorites.

The arrival of Lewis Hallam in 1753, with a letter of recommendation from Governor Dinwiddie of Virginia in his pocket, constitutes a landmark in the history of the stage in New York. Unfortunately for Hallam, the forces of opposition were now at work and he was obliged to appeal through the press to public opinion before a license was granted him. He and his company had come to New York, he said, little imagining that in a city to all appearances so polite as this the

[24] Quoted by Arthur Hornblow, *op. cit.*, I, p. 46.

Muses would be banished, the works of the immortal Shakespeare and others, the greatest geniuses England ever produced, denied admittance among them. This proved effective and on September 17, 1753, he opened with Steele's comedy, *The Conscious Lover.*[25]

In 1758, David Douglass reorganized the Hallam company, with Mrs. Hallam as the star, and, erecting a playhouse on Cruger's Wharf, near the Old Slip, opened with Rowe's *Jane Shore.* The season lasted six weeks, in which eighteen plays were presented, including *Richard III* and *Othello.* A few years later Douglass was back in New York, erecting a new theater at the corner of Nassau and Beekman Streets, where he gave performances of *The Fair Penitent*, *Hamlet*, *Tamerlane*, *Cato*, and *King Henry IV.* Unfortunately, the success of this venture was threatened by the insistence of the city fops upon going on the stage to ogle the actresses, which incensed the audience and brought upon them more than one shower of ancient eggs.[26]

Altogether, New York was fortunate in the enjoyment of many fine plays during the colonial period, presented by talented actors and actresses. Could motion pictures have been made of Mrs. Hallam's portrayals of Juliet, Cordelia, Portia, or Jane Shore, they would no doubt prove her to have been a most capable actress. In her day she was the idol not only of New Yorkers, but of theater patrons wherever she appeared. To the millions who crowd into the splendid theaters which line the great white way of the present, the little playhouses on Nassau Street or Cruger's Wharf would seem primitive indeed, but one wonders whether the performances, however

[25] *New York Gazette*, September 17, 1753.
[26] Arthur Hornblow, *op. cit.*, I, p. 117.

lacking in elaborate accessories and stage setting, were not the equal of the best of today. The colonial audiences at least had the pleasure of seeing Shakespeare's plays presented at frequent intervals, a privilege only too rare in the present sophisticated age.

Colonial New Yorkers also had reason to congratulate themselves upon their opportunities to hear good music. The theatrical companies brought with them a number of musicians, vocal and instrumental, who sang or played between acts, and such favorites as Miss Wainwright or Miss Hallam were always greeted enthusiastically. *The Beggar's Opera, Damon and Phillida,* and other ballad operas were also popular. The first concert of which we have record was given in 1736 for the benefit of a Mr. Pachelbel, a harpsichord player. Other benefit concerts followed, for Charles Love, of the Hallam Company; William Hulett,[27] actor, dancing master, and violinist; Alexander Dienval, who gave lessons on the violin, German flute, hautboy, French horn, and bass violin.[28]

In 1760, musical appreciation in New York had advanced so far that Hulett and Dienval established a series of subscription concerts, which proved remarkably successful and were continued each season for eight years. It was at these concerts that the age-old battle between the music lovers and the conversationalists again flared forth. "I am a dear lover of music and can't bear to be disturbed in my enjoyment," wrote a correspondent to the *Postboy* signing himself "X.Y.Z." "How great then is my disappointment and vexation, when instead of a modest and becoming silence nothing is heard during the whole performance but laughing and talking very loud,

[27] *New York Gazette,* February 26, 1765.
[28] J. T. Howard, *op. cit.,* p. 29.

Theatre flourished

squawling, overturning of benches, etc., behavior more suited to a broglio than a musical entertainment."[29] One wonders whether the audience kept better order when open-air summer concerts were started in Ranelagh Gardens,[30] in the "King's Arms Garden in the Broadway," and in "Vaux Hall Gardens."

Colonial New York owed much to William Tuckey, formerly Vicar Choral of the Bristol Cathedral, who became choirmaster of Trinity Church. Beginning with the pupils of the church charity school, he developed a choir whose fame spread far beyond the city confines. His greatest triumph was the organizing and training of a large chorus which gave the first rendition in America of Handel's *Messiah*, with orchestral accompaniment. Tuckey was also a concert artist. In 1755 he took part in a benefit concert at the New Exchange in which, "among a variety of select pieces both vocal and instrumental," were performed "the celebrated dialogue between Damon and Chloe," *An Ode on Masonry*, and a solo on the German flute. The concert began early in the evening, so that at its conclusion there could be a "ball for the ladies."[31]

Tuckey won distinction also as a composer, but we have no means of judging the merit of his creations since none has come down to us save those in psalm collections. His *Thanksgiving Anthem* was sung before General Amherst to celebrate his triumphal return to New York after the conquest of Canada, and his *Anthem from the Ninety-Seventh Psalm* was rendered at a sacred concert for the benefit of the Pennsylvania Hospital.[32] Had conditions been more favorable, this

[29] *Ibid.*, p. 30.
[30] *New York Gazette*, June 27, 1768.
[31] J. T. Howard, *op. cit.*, pp. 31, 32.
[32] *Ibid.*, p. 32.

remarkable man might have made choral music popular in America decades before the days of the Handel Society of Boston set the standard for the country, but his insistent efforts in the main were futile.

Art in colonial New York found perhaps its finest expression in silver, and Gotham had good reason to be proud of the porringers, tankards, mugs, and coffeepots which came out of the shops of Jacob Boelen, Peter Van Dyke, Benjamin Wynkoop, and other master silversmiths. In the work of these craftsmen, as in architecture, education, and literature, we may follow the struggle between the Dutch and English civilizations and the ultimate victory of the latter.

The early silversmiths were Dutchmen, who followed Dutch patterns and used Dutch methods. When we view one of Garrett Onclebagh's tankards, with its massiveness, its ruggedness, its simplicity, we at once picture the solid Dutch burgher, seated at the tavern drinking liberally of excellent beer. It could never be mistaken for an English tankard. The strain of delicacy in the work of the New York silversmiths which seems foreign to Holland was introduced by a group of Huguenot craftsmen–Bartholomew le Roux, Philip Goelet, Elias Pelletreau, and others. But the French influence was not lasting, and just as the French tongue of the Huguenot and Walloon settlers gave way to Dutch, so French forms and ornamentation in silver gradually disappeared.

The beaker was perhaps the most charming of the early New York pieces, because of the simplicity of its form and decoration. An evolution from the ancient drinking horn, the beaker had superseded the chalice in the Dutch Reformed churches, and so was turned out in comparatively large numbers. Seven inches in height, widening in a graceful curve at the top, decorated with florate designs and with molding around the base, it was practically a duplicate of the beakers of Holland. On the other hand, the tankard was from the first the result of the mingling of cultures, for it was an English product, introduced by English workers, yet so modified as to take on a distinctly Dutch flavor. It became heavier than in England, lower, with plain body, corkscrew thumbpiece, large handle, foliate design encircling the base, and lid decorated with flowers and a cherub's head. Later the straight sides gave way to a graceful bulge. The early New York teapots, though clearly Dutch in origin, took on an individuality of their own, the inverted pear shape, so common in the old country, being toned down, in some cases almost to a sphere. But the shape of the handle, the lid, the character of the decorations were very similar to those of teapots made in Holland.

In New York, as in Boston, some of the silversmiths were men of high social position and influence. Peter Van Dyke served as constable and assessor and took a leading part in all civic activities. As a craftsman he ranks with the best. In no sense a slavish imitator of European models, he stamped each tankard, each porringer, each teapot with his own individuality.

Gradually, with the passing of Van Dyke, Garrett Onclebagh, and other workers of the old school, the Dutch influence declined. Workmen arrived from England, bringing new styles and a new technique; silverware was imported from England to adorn the cupboards of leading New Yorkers and to provide new patterns for the silversmiths. With the second decade of the eighteenth century the English rococo made its appearance in Manhattan, and later, with the classical revival, the Dutch strain died out.

The history of culture in New York during the eighteenth century illustrates in a most interesting way the trend toward a uniform civilization in continental America. In the early decades the town was unique, and to the Bostonian or Philadelphian who came there for business or to visit friends it seemed almost as foreign as Paris or Lisbon. They were startled to see street after street lined with Dutch houses, to hear the people speaking Dutch, to attend services held in Dutch, to find the shops filled with Dutch wares. But a century later New York, to a large extent, had lost its foreign flavor, had become a typical American mercantile city quite similar to Philadelphia or Boston or Norfolk in its architecture, language, educational system, craftsmanship, customs.

The change was brought about in part by the influence of England. From London came the volumes which filled the shelves of the bookshops, the textbooks used in schools and in the college, the works of Gibbs and Halfpenny to remodel architectural ideas, the silversmiths and cabinetmakers who remolded local styles in the artistic crafts. For New York, as well as other colonial cities, London was the great center of culture, whose dictates none dared disobey.

But there were also powerful intercolonial forces at work. Wedged in between the English of New England on the one side and the English of New Jersey and Pennsylvania on the other, New York was deeply influenced by both. Connecticut Yankees were constantly sending their little vessels down into the East River laden with farm produce for exchange for the imported goods displayed in the shops of Broad or Pearl Streets; New Jersey as far south as New Brunswick was commercially tributary to the New York merchants. On Long Island and in Westchester the New Englanders had planted themselves within a few miles of the city, bringing with them not only their language and religion, but their architecture, schools, farming methods, traditions, and crafts.

There was increasing contact, also, with the more remote colonies. Hardly a day passed without the coming of a schooner or brig from Charleston, or the Chesapeake Bay, or the clearing of a vessel for Newport or Boston. Travel by land was far more frequent than formerly, and the improvement of the roads, the erection of bridges, the institution of stagecoach and ferry services made it possible for travelers from Philadelphia to reach the city in a day and a half.[33] Intermarriage between New York families and Bostonians or Philadelphians proved a strong link with those cities and a force for a more cosmopolitan culture, and when a Quaker City, or Maryland, or Boston lass married a New Yorker and came to Gotham to live, she no doubt did her bit to strengthen English styles and social customs. One is reminded that this was not an infrequent occurrence by the fact that the Wendells of New York were related to the Quincys, Sewalls, and Hancocks of Massachusetts, the DeLanceys to the Allens of Philadelphia, the Wards of Philadelphia to the Wards of New York, etc.[34]

The intercolonial spirit in New York was fostered by the various religious denominations. It is true that the Reformed Church had originally been national in scope, and had battled strenuously for the preservation of the Dutch tongue and culture. But Frelinghuysen and other leading ministers, early recognizing the need of support from other Calvinist groups, fraternized with German Reformed and Presbyterians and welcomed the great evangelist George Whitefield to their pulpits. So close was the friendship between Princeton and these men that they sent some of their most promising youths there to study under Burr or Davies, and after the Revolution seriously considered uniting their own college at New Brunswick

[33] Wheaton J. Lane, *From Indian Trail to Iron Horse* (Princeton, N. J.: Princeton University Press, 1939), p. 128.

[34] Michael Kraus, *op. cit.*, pp. 43, 44.

with it. As for the New York Presbyterians and Episcopalians, they were, of course, closely tied to the Presbyterians and Episcopalians of other colonies.

Even the theater tended to break down provincialism, not only by giving New Yorkers a new appreciation of the great English dramatists and so weaning them from the Dutch writers, but by bringing them into line with other American cities. The theater in America was intercolonial, not local. Printing, also, had its effect, for the gazettes found their way into all the provinces, and the more interesting articles were reprinted for local consumption. In this way New Yorkers learned what was going on in Massachusetts or South Carolina and so became more appreciative of the culture and the spirit of those colonies.

It must not be imagined that New York, even at the close of the eighteenth century, had lost entirely its Dutch flavor. Old Grant Thorburn declared that when he "stept on shore at Governeur's wharf" in 1794, "Dutch houses, Dutch goods, Dutch manners, Dutch words, Dutch men and Dutch lasses were much in vogue." The Washington Market was still supplied from the surrounding Dutch farms, and unless you understood Dutch it was useless to try to trade there.[35] Yet this was but the last gasp of a waning culture, for already New York had become chiefly English and American. The few remaining Dutch preachers, the one or two Dutch schools, the scattered Dutch houses were but reminders of a past age, signposts pointing not to the future but to the past. It was the New York of the Livingstons, William Smith, and Cadwallader Colden which was to pass over into the nineteenth century and become the metropolis of America.

[35] *Princeton Whig*, July 11, 1845.

CULTURE WITH A "THEE AND A THOU"

Philadelphia

WHEN William Penn founded his colony on the banks of the Delaware, he envisioned a planned civilization. He and the Society of Friends were to put into practice ideals which were to permeate the life of the people and fix the character not only of religious practice, but of the government, social customs, education, art. Less rigid than the Wilderness Zion of Massachusetts, milder in its concept of human relations, based on freedom of religion, it was not the less powerful. His Holy Experiment, Penn called it.

The Quakers had no church to serve as an intermediary between the individual and his Maker, no priesthood, no church buildings. They insisted upon rigid morality, but it was enforced more by admonition than by stern laws. They condemned war as unnecessary and unchristian; believed that deference to rank and position was contrary to the will of God; greeted all men with the familiar "thou" and refused to take off their hats in the presence of judges or even kings; carried their condemnation of ostentation even into the graveyard, where tombstones were plain and simple; frowned on costly dress, pretentious residences, ornate furniture and silver.

The Friends believed in primary and grammar schools, and established many that did excellent work. But they saw no need for higher education, and Penn had been dead a century before they founded their first college. So long as their views dominated the Philadelphia region, the life of the mind was not apt to flourish; it was not apt to produce a group of distinguished scientists and men of letters. As for the field of theological disputation, the lack of an established clergy doomed it to sterility from the first.

In other cultural fields, also, Quaker principles proved a severe handicap. Music was regarded with suspicion as a sensuous enjoyment which beclouded the realities of life. The theater was forbidden. Since plainness and simplicity were the marks of the true Christian, one must beware of pretentious houses set off with costly ornamentation; fine dress for men and for women was a mark of frivolity; costly furniture and silver were unnecessary and extravagant. In other words, Quakerism, so far as it maintained its moral influence, was a handicap to the development of architecture, the artistic crafts, music, and the theater.

But Quakerism, although it maintained throughout the colonial period its political ascendency, gradually lost its grip upon the minds of a large part of the population. From a very early date it had to struggle against two growing forces—the development of wealth and the influence of the non-Quaker elements of the population.

The early Quaker settlers were yeomen, most of them, coming from various parts of the British Isles—the midland counties, London, Bristol, Yorkshire, Wales, Ulster.[1] Farmers most of them remained after they settled in Pennsylvania, although their new acres far outnumbered the old. The colony had been in existence but a few years when they began to pour their produce into the Philadelphia market—wheat, barley, rye,

[1] Isaac Sharpless, "The Quakers in Pennsylvania," in Rufus M. Jones, *The Quakers in the American Colonies* (London: The Macmillan Company, 1911), pp. 422, 440.

Indian corn, fruits, meat. "Our lands have been grateful to us and have begun to reward our labors with abounding crops of corn," wrote one settler enthusiastically.

But many remained in Philadelphia, to build wharves and warehouses along the river front and devote themselves to the mercantile life. Upon them, even more than upon the farmers, fortune cast her smiles. In a surprisingly short time the city became a busy trading center, receiving the produce of the surrounding country and shipping it out to various parts of the world. George Horworth reported in 1715 that the town was about a mile long, held a market twice a week, was full of "country business and sea affairs," and the river crowded with ships and sloops.[2] As early as 1690 a lucrative trade had sprung up with the West Indies. "I understand ten or twelve sail went loaden thither last summer with biscuit, flour, beef and pork," wrote Richard Morris.[3] One number of the *Pennsylvania Gazette*, in 1758, reported vessels entering from New York, Rhode Island, Boston, and Montserrat, and clearing for Antigua, Jamaica, Barbados, Belfast, Newry, and St. Christopher. In 1772 we find brigs, ships, sloops, snows, and schooners trading to Cadiz, Boston, Dublin, St. Croix, Virginia, Santo Domingo, Madeira, Liverpool, Londonderry, and other places.[4]

With the accumulation of wealth came the temptation to forget the old, simple life and to indulge in fine clothes, build handsome houses, and live luxuriously. As this tendency grew, the Quaker organization combated it by drawing up and enforcing rigid rules of discipline. The Quaker who indulged in "costly attire, foolish dresses and new fashions, ruffling, peri-

[2] *Pennsylvania Magazine*, XXXVII, pp. 330–340.
[3] *Ibid.*, IV, pp. 189–201.
[4] *Pennsylvania Gazette*, June 25, 1772.

wigs, needless buttons, wide skirts and long flat-sleeved coats,"[5] or laid out his money in silver teapots and spoons, or in costly furniture was sure to receive a warning from the Meeting. In the face of this severity many took refuge in conservatism, extolling the virtues of the early generation and turning their backs upon temptation, but an increasing minority, refusing to have their lives thus regulated, remained Quakers only in name, and turned with zest to the enjoyment of intellectual and cultural pleasures.

They found ardent allies in the growing non-Quaker population in Philadelphia, especially the Scottish and English merchants who moved to the city to join in its increasing trade. These men, many of them affiliated with the Church of England, built handsome residences in the city or its suburbs, laid out beautiful gardens, purchased the tables and highboys of Affleck, Randolph, and Savory, lent their support to the new college, were patrons of science, purchased large libraries, saw no harm in attending a performance of *Othello* or *Hamlet*, spread a bountiful table, rode in fine coaches, delighted in the minuet. Together, these non-Quakers and nonconformist Quakers gave Philadelphia a cultural life of which any city might have been proud.

They were ably seconded by that versatile genius, Benjamin Franklin—statesman, diplomat, writer, publisher, postmaster, scientist, soldier, philosopher, civil leader. There was little love lost between this plebeian, New England printer-tradesman and the elect and exclusive Philadelphia aristocracy, and, even when Franklin had been admitted to the most select circles of Europe, there were certain old Tory ladies in Philadelphia who turned up their noses at him. Yet he was in full accord

[5] *Pennsylvania Magazine*, VII, p. 354.

with the more enlightened in encouraging higher education, stimulating scientific investigation, bettering the general appreciation of art, music, and architecture. Every forward-looking scheme—for a college, for a public library, for a philosophical society, for a hospital—either originated in his fertile brain or had his hearty support.[6]

It is only within recent years that R. T. H. Halsey has drawn attention to Franklin's love of music, poetry, the graphic arts, architecture, pottery, and painting. Himself a musician and adept with the guitar, harp, violin, and harmonica, he had no sympathy with the Quaker suspicion of fine music. From his early youth he enjoyed poetry, and in after life even his strong dislike of Dr. Samuel Johnson did not prevent him from reading his works. Himself a skilled engraver, Franklin was an ardent collector of fine engravings and a friend of William Hogarth, the Abbé de Saint-Non, and other artists. He was deeply interested, also, in pottery, and it was he who suggested "the printing of square tiles for ornamenting chimneys from copper plates."[7]

Franklin was the real founder of the college which expanded into the University of Pennsylvania. At the time there were but four colleges in the colonies, Harvard, William and Mary, Yale, and Princeton, and Franklin, in a published prospectus, appealed to the Philadelphians to found still another, in their own city. Taking over a vacant building erected several years earlier for a charity school which had been planned but had not materialized, the trustees opened classes in 1751, and Provost William Smith inaugurated regular college courses four years later. This institution from the first affected pro-

[6] *See* Vernon L. Parrington, *op. cit.*, pp. 164–178.

[7] R. T. Haines Halsey, *Benjamin Franklin and His Circle* (New York: Metropolitan Museum of Art, 1936), pp. 1–16.

foundly the intellectual and cultural life of the middle colonies and had the honor of establishing the first chair of botany and natural history and of initiating the first systematic instruction in medicine.[8]

From the first the college had the advantage of drawing upon many excellent schools for a body of well-prepared youths. Oldest of these was the George Keith's School, now the William Penn Charter School, which did good work throughout the colonial period. There were also schools established by the Quakers in most of the rural districts, to which poor scholars were admitted free of charge, so that a grammar-school education was within the reach of all save those living on the frontiers.[9] Among the Philadelphia schoolmasters were David James Dove, Simon Williams, William Dawson, Joseph Garner, Thomas Pratt, Enoch Flower, Thomas Lloyd, and Pelatiah Webster.

Dove, the first English teacher in Franklin's Academy, was described as an excellent master who had taught sixteen years in England. However, one of his pupils stigmatized him as "a sarcastic and ill-tempered doggerelizer, who was but ironically Dove, for his temper was that of a hawk, and his pen the beak of a falcon pouncing on his prey."[10] Dove later became English master at the Germantown Academy, and, when his ungovernable temper had forced the trustees to dismiss him, refused to yield possession of the school building to his successor. It is said that Dove rarely used the birch upon the back of a delinquent student, but stuck it in the collar behind

[8] The claim that this college established the first law school in America is not valid, for it was antedated by Wythe's law school at William and Mary.

[9] Isaac Sharpless, *op. cit.*, pp. 527, 528.

[10] John T. Faris, *The Romance of Old Philadelphia* (Philadelphia: J. B. Lippincott Company, 1918), pp. 156–160.

his neck, so that he had to go through with his exercises with this badge of disgrace towering over his head.[11]

The methods used and the subjects taught in the Philadelphia schools are set forth in the advertisements in the gazettes. Simon Williams promised that children who had not yet learned the elements of English would be taught to pronounce and read properly "in a manner most easy to themselves. Young gentlemen who have made any tolerable progress in the English language will be taught the art of fair writing, merchants' accounts and a grammatical knowledge of their mother tongue, as it is judiciously laid down in Greenwood's *English Grammar*. A compendious system of practical mathematics consisting of some books of the elements of Euclid, trigonometry and practical geometry. The knowledge of the Greek and Latin tongues, including the most valuable authors of the Roman Classics. And, lastly, the following sciences, namely geography, rhetoric, poetry, history, moral philosophy and physics."[12]

In science, as in education, it was Franklin who took the lead. He it was who organized the Junto, that interesting group which met once a week to discuss the nature of "vapors" or of sound over their beer and pipes. In 1769 the Junto was merged with a rival society to form the American Philosophical Society, with Franklin as its first president. Modeled after the Royal Society, it differed from it in the emphasis placed upon America, its natural resources, and possible improvements in "agriculture, farming and gardening." But it also promised to devote itself to "other useful subjects, either in physics, mechanics, astronomy, mathematics, etc." Its chief hope lay in "encouraging and directing inquiries and experi-

[11] *Ibid.*, p. 160.
[12] *Pennsylvania Gazette*, August 2, 1759.

ments, receiving, collecting and digesting discoveries, inventions and improvements, communicating them to the public and distinguishing their authors."[13]

Not only was Franklin organizer and president of the Society, but by far its ablest and most versatile scientist, his interests embracing electricity, astronomy, mathematics, medicine, invention, meteorology, oceanography, and a dozen other fields of research. His discoveries in electricity were received with astonishment by European scientists. "Nothing was ever written upon the subject of electricity which was more generally read and admired in all parts of Europe," wrote Dr. Priestley. America, the frontier, the outpost of civilization, had produced a scientist of the first rank. Franklin was awarded the Copley medal in 1753, was elected fellow of the Royal Society in 1756, and given honorary degrees by the universities of Edinburgh, Oxford, and St. Andrews.

His most famous contribution was the demonstration that electricity and lightning are identical. Improvising a kite by covering two cross sticks with a silk handkerchief, he affixed an iron point, and added a long hempen string, to the lower end of which he tied a key. Upon the approach of a thundercloud he raised the kite, retreated under a shed, and awaited results. For some time no sign of electricity was observable and Franklin was beginning to fear that his experiment would prove a failure. Then, suddenly, he noted that the loose fibers of his string were becoming erect, and presenting his knuckle to the key he received a strong spark. One of the most dramatic experiments in the history of science had proved successful.[14]

Less versatile than Franklin, but the embodiment of the

[13] *Transactions* of the American Philosophical Society, I, XV–XIX.
[14] Fred E. Brasch, in *The Scientific Monthly*, XXXIII.

pioneer spirit in science, was the self-taught astronomer, David Rittenhouse. How irrepressible is the scientific spirit even under the most discouraging conditions is shown by the eagerness of this farmer boy to devour every book on mathematics he could lay his hands on, and by his habit of covering plow handles, fences, stones, and barn doors with figures and constellations. Rittenhouse constructed an orrery in 1767 which was purchased by Princeton College. This marvelous machine, with its three faces showing the solar system, Jupiter and its satellites, and the phases of the moon, survived the occupation of Nassau Hall successively by British and American troops during the Revolution. Rittenhouse won fame for his study of the transit of Venus, his discovery of an atmosphere on Venus, his measurement of the distance to the sun, and his study of the transit of Mercury.

Other members of the remarkable scientific group of Philadelphians were John Morgan, father of medical education in America; the botanist, John Bartram; the ornithologists, John J. Audubon and Alexander Wilson; Benjamin Rush, William Shippen, Thomas Bond, and other distinguished physicians. The Pennsylvania Hospital set a new standard in efficiency and enlightened methods for the colonies and led the way in its treatment of the insane as sufferers rather than criminals. In all, it was a splendid record of scientific accomplishment for a community which a few decades before had been planted in a wilderness, a record equaled by none of the other colonies.

In providing the facilities for reading, as in so many other things, Franklin was the leader, and his Library Company of Philadelphia set the pace for an epoch of library building in the colonies comparable to that of the Carnegie library movement more than a century later. Between the years 1745 and

1763 no less than seventeen were founded, of which one third were located in Pennsylvania, including the Library of Friends, the Union Library, Amicable Library, and Association Library. We gain an insight into the workings of these institutions from a notice published by the Directors of the Juliana Library Company of Lancaster. All members in arrears with their dues were to be dropped and their shares declared forfeited. Those who kept in their possession "any of the company's books, mathematical instruments and other effects" beyond the allotted time were to be dealt with severely. "The value of the company's effects, by several late importations and generous donations, is greatly increased and any vacancies that may happen by the expulsion of the delinquents will without doubt speedily be filled."[15]

Persons wishing to build up private libraries, or to purchase single volumes, could do so by visiting one of the local bookstores—David Hall's at the new printing office, Market Street; or John Bleakley's, at the Sign of the Three Bibles; or James Rivington's, on Front Street; or R. Aitkin's opposite the London Coffee House. Here one had a wide selection—Drummond's *Travels*, Milton's *Works*, Hutchinson's *System of Moral Philosophy*, Brook's *Practice of Physic*, *Every Man His Own Lawyer*, Whiston's *Josephus*, *Pallein on Silk-worms*, *Builder's Dictionary*, *History of Herodotus*, Grove's *Sermons*, Buchanan's *History of Scotland*, *The Spectator*, Prior's *Poems*, *The Tatler*, *The Rambler*, Molière's *Works*, Shakespeare's *Works*, Addison's *Works*, Swift's *Works*, Pope's *Poems*, etc.[16]

It was a movement of tremendous moment, this rapid expansion of reading in the colonies in the third quarter of the eighteenth century. It molded literary taste; had a profound

[15] *Pennsylvania Gazette*, January 6, 1773. [16] *Ibid.*, March 15, 1759.

effect in preparing the ground for the American Revolution by acquainting a wide group with the works of Montesquieu, Voltaire, Rousseau, and other European writers; stimulated interest in the theater, architecture, painting, and music; brought to a wide circle the culture which formerly had been confined to the few; subjected the colonies more closely to English cultural domination, yet loosened forces which were to lead to a large degree of independence. The time was not yet ripe for the intellectual democracy dreamed of by Jefferson, but the libraries and bookstores of the mid-eighteenth century were the prelude for the mass education of the nineteenth.

The widened scope of reading was attended by a rising body of publication. "There were [no writers] in the first twenty years of the colony, the struggle with nature being too imperious," it was said. "But the second generation, relieved from the toil of settlement in the forest, . . . and reaping plenty from rich and bountiful fields, cleared by the labor of their fathers, first turned their eyes to Heaven in thankfulness, and then to Parnassus for inspiration to celebrate the beauty and delights of their happy country."[17] In the pages of the gazettes and almanacs appeared the outpourings of amateur poets. And although most of it was unharmonious, inelegant, and spiritless, a few had sprightliness and grace. James Logan wrote Latin verses and Greek odes, while Aquila Rose, the first Philadelphia poet to attract attention, surprises us by the beauty of his creations.[18]

In journalism the remarkable Franklin, as usual, was the leader not only in Philadelphia but throughout America, for

[17] John T. Scharf and Thompson Wescott, *History of Philadelphia* (Philadelphia: L. H. Everts and Company, 1884), I, p. 225.

[18] *Ibid.*, pp. 202, 225, 226.

he made his own paper a model for others, while he was instrumental in financing papers in several colonies. His *Pennsylvania Gazette* in form differed little from the typical colonial sheet, its news columns being devoted chiefly to European affairs, mixed in with a few local items such as poems, letters, or discussions of city or provincial problems, many interesting advertisements, and occasional reprints from the English writers. Had it had no other function than serving as a mouthpiece for Franklin himself, the *Gazette* would have been an important sheet.

The local presses were kept busy with the republication of popular English books. In 1774 James Humphreys, Jr., printer on Front Street, begged the subscribers to Sterne's *Works* to be patient, as an unlucky accident and the "great scarcity of careful workmen" had delayed its appearance several weeks.[19] John Dunlap reprinted Oliver Goldsmith's *She Stoops to Conquer*, of which he thought it necessary to state: "This play is truly comic, the humor is irresistible and pleases in the closet as well as in the theatre."[20] The colonial equivalent of the modern "horror" stories were the "hell-fire sermons" of Gilbert Tennent[21] and other New Light preachers and the thrilling accounts of Indian adventures. Typical was "*A Narrative of the Sufferings and Surprising Deliverance of William and Elizabeth Fleming*, who were taken captives by Captain Jacobs in a late excursion by him and the Indians under his command."[22]

In 1741 Franklin made a new and important venture by putting out the *General Magazine and Historical Chronicle For All The British Plantations in America*. This was an expression

[19] *Pennsylvania Gazette*, March 2, 1774.
[20] *Ibid.*, August 18, 1773.
[21] *Ibid.*, August 24, 1758.
[22] *Ibid.*, February 19, 1756.

of intercolonial solidarity which may be considered a forerunner to Franklin's Albany Plan for political union. The magazine made a point of reprinting essays, poems, and other items not from the English journals, but from American gazettes. Its department of "Accounts of or Extracts from new books, pamphlets, etc. published in the plantations" is the first real attempt at book reviewing in the colonies.[23]

After surveying the many cultural fields in which Franklin took the lead in Philadelphia, one is almost startled to find that in architecture the city could attain distinction without his especial guidance. Like Jefferson, Franklin was a scientist, statesman, diplomat, musician, but, unlike the Virginian, he was not a great architect. It was the good taste of the average wealthy Philadelphian, the common interest in architecture of the cultured group, the presence of the Carpenters' Company, that society of able architects and builders, and the custom of referring to English books on architecture that gave the community the most remarkable group of civic buildings in colonial America, the most beautiful church structure, and scores of handsome residences.

Philadelphia was the first Renaissance city in America, for it was built at a period when all England was thrilled by the restoration of London after the terrible fire of 1666. Visitors to the town which was arising between the Delaware and the Schuylkill invariably declared that it was built "after the London way," and for decades Market Street or High Street were almost replicas of Cheapside or Cannon or Thames Streets. "The houses are all of brick," declared Governor Thomas Pownall, "the fronts of them precisely such as those in Cheapside, London; a pent over the base story and shops, and a little

[23] James Truslow Adams, *Provincial Society* (New York: The Macmillan Company, 1927), p. 269.

slip of a window to light a closet by the side of the chimneys."[24]

Yet in a few years the Quakers so modified this British inheritance by infusing into it something of their own sincerity and simplicity as to create a distinctly Philadelphia architecture. The charming meetinghouses, some of brick, but many of rough stone, with their hooded doors and multipaned windows, breathe the very spirit of Quakerism, whereas the little Letitia house, now moved to Fairmount Park where it overlooks the Schuylkill, is as characteristically early Philadelphian as the Adam Thoroughgood house is Virginian, or the House of the Seven Gables a product of Massachusetts.

It was in the mid-eighteenth century that the early Quaker style began to give way to the Georgian. Members of the Carpenters' Company altered their ideas to conform to the designs shown in the books of Gibbs, Halfpenny, Langley, and others; English architects moved to Philadelphia and proudly announced that they were prepared to design houses according to the "modern taste"; Dr. John Kearsley, Andrew Hamilton, and other gifted amateurs became enamored of the new style. But these men, while accepting the Georgian as a basis for their work, added so much of their own individuality, so much of the spirit of the community itself, that they created what may aptly be termed the Philadelphia Georgian. Characterized by the constant use of Palladian windows, by ornate dormers, the Doric entrance door, elbowed mantels, marble bands, and flat arches, one recognizes it at a glance. We find it at its best in famous old Cliveden, or Mount Pleasant, or Landowne.[25]

The fine residences of Philadelphia and its suburbs were

[24] *Pennsylvania Magazine*, XVIII, pp. 211–218.

[25] Thomas J. Wertenbaker, *The Founding of American Civilization—The Middle Colonies* (New York: Charles Scribner's Sons, 1938), pp. 243–246.

furnished in large part with tables, highboys, and chairs made by local cabinetmakers. These skilled craftsmen were not subjected to the competition of English workers, which proved so devastating in the South, for trade directly with the mother country was not so extensive and cargo space was dearer. It was this which made possible the development of a group of artists in wood inferior to none, not even those of London itself.

The men who set up shop on Market Street or Church Alley in the early days of the city were Englishmen who brought with them English patterns, traditions, and methods of work. They began in Philadelphia just where they had left off in London or Bristol. Yet local conditions, the simplicity of Quaker life, the cheapness of black walnut, the dearness of labor immediately began to affect their work and to give it a character of its own. When Benjamin Randolph got an order for a table or highboy, he turned to his book of models for the lines, ornaments, and inlay, but he made no exact reproductions, so that each piece was his own creation.

The early furniture reflected the Quaker ideals. "Be careful to avoid all superfluity of furniture," the orthodox Quaker was warned, and the presence in his house of ornate chairs and tables was sure to excite criticism. In time the Philadelphia cabinetmakers became more subservient to prevailing English styles, but even in the Queen Anne period, which in America continued through the third decade of the eighteenth century, the grotesque birds and baroque shells, common in England, fortunately were unknown in the local shops.

The golden era of the Philadelphia cabinetmakers, when Thomas Affleck, Benjamin Randolph, Jonathan Gostelowe, and other masters turned out their beautiful Chippendale highboys, secretary-bookcases, lowboys, tables, and chairs, ran

cabinet makers

from midcentury to the beginning of the Federalist period. These pieces were based on Chippendale's *The Gentleman and Cabinetmaker's Directory*, but each had its own individuality, was a masterpiece of workmanship. Characterized by beautiful curves, carved splats, cabriole legs, ball and claw feet, broken pediments, and rich ornamentation with Gothic figures or foliage and flowers, they would have done honor to Hampton Court itself.[26]

As the influence of Chippendale in England yielded to that of Sir William Chambers and the Adam brothers, the Philadelphia cabinetmakers turned with enthusiasm first to the Marlborough style with its straight legs and plinth and its Gothic or classical carving, and later to the Sheraton and Hepplewhite styles. Through succeeding periods they retained their ascendency in the colonies, not only supplying the local market, but shipping their pieces to Maryland, Virginia, and even the West Indies. Later, however, when their shops developed into little factories, having their specialists for each task—carvers, inlayers, turners, upholsterers—the output became stereotyped and lifeless, a joint product rather than the creation of one master hand.[27]

Philadelphia had reason to be proud of her silversmiths not less than her cabinetmakers, for the Richardson family, the Syng family, Richard Humphreys, Christian Wiltberger, and others did work which was of the highest artistry and workmanship. In fact, the development of silverwork in the city also paralleled closely that of cabinetmaking. Choosing Euro-

[26] William M. Hornor, *Blue Book of Philadelphia Furniture* (Philadelphia, 1935).

[27] *A Picture Book of Philadelphia Chippendale Furniture* (Philadelphia: Pennsylvania Museum of Art, 1931); *Authenticated Furniture of the Great Philadelphia Cabinetmakers* (Philadelphia: Pennsylvania Museum of Art, 1935).

pean models, the Quaker craftsman in the early days modified them so as to attain extreme simplicity of form, although this often robbed the tankards and mugs of much of their beauty. Later, wealthy Philadelphians began to demand porringers, teapots, tankards, candlesticks, and other pieces whose grace and delicacy would harmonize with the elaborate finish and furnishings of their houses. In response, the silversmiths, using English books of design as the basis of their work, began to turn out silver characterized by the finest workmanship.[28]

The history of silver in colonial Philadelphia revolves around the Richardsons and the Syngs. Francis Richardson, whose shop was at the corner of Letitia Court and Market Street, seems to have paid more attention to watchmaking than to silversmithing, but his son Joseph and grandsons Joseph and Nathaniel turned out scores of pieces as fine as any in colonial America. Fortunately, the daybook of the elder Joseph has been preserved, and it gives a welcome insight into work done by the local craftsmen. Now he enters to the account of Israel Pemberton, Jr, a gold girdle buckle, six teaspoons, tongs and strainer, two porringers, one set of castors, one waiter, and a pair of silver buckles; now he charges Jane Fenn with a pair of shoeclasps, a strainer, a soup spoon, a pair of salts, and six teaspoons; now Caspar Wistar with four porringers, a pepper box, a pair of salts, four buttons, and a pair of knee buckles.[29]

The work of the Syng family was in no way inferior to that of the Richardsons, while their position in Philadelphia life was more important. Philip Syng was a close friend of Franklin, first Master of the Mint, a member of the American Philosophical Society, a director of the Library Company of Philadelphia, an original trustee of the Academy, a leader in

[28] *Pennsylvania Museum Bulletin*, No. 68.

[29] *Pennsylvania Magazine*, XXIX, pp. 121–122.

"actors were little above criminals"

civic affairs. His mugs with their shapely handles and gracefully bulging bodies, his famous inkstand used at the signing of the Declaration of Independence and the Constitution, his porringers, and other pieces rank with the best in America. Nor did the Richardsons and Syngs have a monopoly of silversmithing, for William Ball, in his shop on Front Street, William Vallant, John Letelier, John David, and others were also doing good work. The heyday of the Philadelphia silversmiths came with the last quarter of the century, when Richard Humphreys, Christian Wiltberger, Joseph Lownes, John Letelier, Edmond Milne, and many others turned out well-proportioned tankards, graceful tea and coffee services, and artistic cream pitchers, and not until the early years of the nineteenth century did the city lose its preëminence in this artistic craft.[30]

Though the Philadelphian could build a fine residence and fill it with costly furniture and silver, a storm of protest greeted him when he tried to attend a performance at the theater. Not only did the Quakers place actors on a level very little above criminals, but they regarded all plays, even Shakespeare's plays, as immoral and tending to vanity and corruption. In this they were heartily supported by the New Light Presbyterians, and the quiet condemnation of the Quaker meetings was ably seconded by the thunderous sermons of Gilbert Tennent. Had it not been for the King, who repeatedly vetoed the laws pushed through the Assembly by these two groups prohibiting plays, there would have been no theater in Pennsylvania.

Great was the horror of all "good people" when it was announced in 1749 that the tragedy *Cato* was to be performed in William Plumstead's warehouse in Water Street alley, and many were the expressions of "sorrow that anything of the kind was encouraged." But the real battle opened only with

[30] *Pennsylvania Museum Bulletin*, No. 68.

the arrival of the Hallams in 1754. Immediately the city was divided into two camps. When a petition was handed in to Governor Hamilton urging him to bar all "prophane stage plays," the more liberal minded countered with another asking that the visiting actors be unmolested. All this noise proved excellent advertisement, so that when Hamilton gave his consent to any performances which were not "indecent or immoral," the crude theater was crowded to overflowing. Opening with *The Fair Penitent* and *Miss in Her Teens*, the troupe continued with *The Gamester*, Rowe's *Tamerlane*, *The Careless Husband*, and other plays.

The storm blew up again, with greater violence than ever, when a proposal was made to erect a theater on the south side of South Street, and so beyond the jurisdiction of the Quaker municipal government, just outside the city limits. The Friends, the Presbyterian Synod, the Lutherans, the Baptists poured in their protests, and the General Assembly once more passed a law forbidding acting under a penalty of a ruinous fine. But, as usual, the King interposed his veto and the theater opened triumphantly before an enthusiastic audience. So successful was this venture that a new theater on South Street, above Fourth Street, was erected in 1766, its Palladian window and cupola giving it somewhat the appearance of a meetinghouse and no doubt adding to the indignation of the pious. Here were presented *Hamlet*, *The Merchant of Venice*, *King Lear*, *The Taming of the Shrew*, *She Stoops to Conquer*, and many other plays. It was only in 1789, however, when the State Legislature, despite bitter opposition from the forces of conservatism, passed an act legalizing plays, that the century-old struggle came to an end.[31]

[31] Thomas J. Wertenbaker, *op. cit.*, pp. 203–205; Arthur Hornblow, *op. cit.*, I, pp. 56, 57, 93–96; *Pennsylvania Gazette*, January 6, 1773, October 25, 1759, etc.

At the theater one had the pleasure of listening to excellent music. When *Macbeth* was presented in 1759 it was announced that "the whole original music as set by Purcell" would be given. At a play in June 1767, Mr. Wooll and Miss Wainwright sang *God Save the King* at the end of Act I, Miss Wainwright sang *The Spinning Wheel* at the end of Act II, there was a duet celebrating the marriage of the Princess Augusta and the Prince of Brunswick at the end of Act III, while Miss Wainwright sang *Lovely Nancy* at the end of Act IV.[32] Plays such as *Theodosius*, *Lethe*, or *Romeo and Juliet* were interspersed with dirges, songs, marches, etc. The opera was always popular, especially the oft-repeated *Beggar's Opera*, which was sure to draw an enthusiastic audience. Other favorites were *Midas*, *Lionel and Clarissa*, *Honest Yorkshireman*, *Padlock Neptune*, and *Amphitrite and Flora*.[33]

Public concerts were rare even in Europe during the mid-century decades, and for Philadelphia music lovers they were few and far between. Yet in 1783 John Bentley presented a series of twelve orchestral concerts which set a high precedent both in the character of the music and the skill of the performers. Music in colonial days, as in America today, had an international flavor and orchestras embraced various nationalities, with German predominating. The programs were modeled after those of England in which overtures and symphonies alternated with songs and instrumental solos and airs from operas. Handel and Haydn were especially popular, but Stamitz, Corelli, and others were not neglected.

It seems strange that Philadelphia, where William Penn and the Quaker meetings condemned music as "frivolous and redolent of the sensuous," should have produced the greatest

[32] Oscar G. Sonneck, *Early Opera in America* (New York: G. Schirmer, 1915), p. 38.

[33] *Ibid.*, pp. 47–50.

American colonial musician in Francis Hopkinson. Beginning the study of the harpsichord at the comparatively late age of seventeen, he never became a great performer, although all who heard him testify to his skill and good taste. Perhaps his chief claim to fame is the improvement he made in the harpsichord by substituting quills of velvet cord for crow quills. So deeply did contemporary musicians appreciate this contribution that they spoke of Hopkinson as "the last glory of the harpsichord."[34]

Philadelphia could claim Benjamin Franklin as her own, although he was not born there; on the other hand, Benjamin West, although born near the city, left for Europe when a mere youth and spent most of his life in England. West, the son of a Quaker innkeeper, early manifested a talent for drawing, although as a child he had never seen a painting, and it was only after friendly Indians showed him their method of mixing war paint that he could color his early efforts at drawing. In 1760, backed by two patrons, he went to Italy, then the center of the artistic world, to study the works of the great masters. When shown the *Apollo Belvedere*, he exclaimed in admiration, "How like a Mohawk warrior!" But his Quaker spirit revolted against Italian Renaissance art, and, though he was the recipient of every courtesy in Italy, he turned his back on that country and moved to London.

Here extraordinary success attended him and his fortune was made when he won the close friendship of George III, a friendship which survived even the American Revolution. It was the King who suggested the painting of *The Departure of Regulus from Rome*, and who actually read the story to West from Livy. Recognizing that with such backing the young American could do wonders for art in England, the painting

[34] Oscar G. Sonneck, *Francis Hopkinson* (privately printed, 1905).

fraternity turned to him for leadership, rallying around the Royal Academy of which he was one of the founders and later president. In 1771 it was noised about London that West had turned to the painting of modern historical scenes and that he was about to break all precedents by using contemporary costumes in his *The Death of Wolfe*. Amid the general dismay, the King, Reynolds, and others begged him not to descend to "boot and breeches" pictures, but he persisted and in so doing brought about a revolution in art.

Although West became an English painter, America influenced his work throughout his life, while he in turn influenced American art profoundly. He never forgot his early lessons when as an untaught youth he was trying to express the strivings and dreams of the "wilderness child"; and his native forests, the Quaker spirit, and the self-reliance and democracy of America affected his work to the last. When he had become the most influential artist in England, he proved a father and guide to every young American painter who knocked at his door—Copley, Stuart, Charles Willson Peale, Rembrandt Peale, Trumbull, and others. A son of America, though not an American painter, West became the father of American painting.

As we review the story of colonial Philadelphia, it becomes apparent that Quakerism was both an obstacle and an aid to the development of culture. Quaker indifference to higher education and hostility to music and the theater tended to impede the progress of the Muses, but its toleration cleared the way for them. As it was a Puritan attack upon freedom of thought which cost Boston the greatest man produced by the American colonies, so it was Quaker liberality which brought him to Philadelphia. Had the Friends slammed the door in the face of newcomers who were of other faiths, had they persecuted those who were not in harmony with their pacifism, their refusal to take oaths, their simple dress and manners, the City of Brotherly Love would not have become in less than a century after its founding a chief center of colonial culture, the home of science, literature, music, the artistic crafts, medicine, and architecture.

INTELLECTUAL LIFE AROUND THE PUNCH BOWL

Annapolis

IT WAS a group of Puritans, driven out of Virginia in 1648 by the intolerance of Sir William Berkeley, who first settled the Annapolis region. And though for decades they clung tenaciously to their distinctive views and even tried to force them on their fellow colonists, in the end they succumbed to the economic and social forces of the region. Living on plantations and not in agricultural villages, remote from both church and school, they gradually freed themselves alike from the Puritan clergy and from Puritan traditions and became part and parcel of the tobacco civilization of the South. William Eddis and others who visited Annapolis at the end of the colonial period could not guess that the gay, sophisticated society in which they found themselves had its origin in a group of Puritans exiled for religion's sake.

The town itself was founded by that professional English governor, Sir Francis Nicholson, who gained such notoriety in a half-dozen colonies for his violent temper, his deep interest in the Anglican Church, his quarrels, his love affairs, and withal his administrative ability and his efforts to crush privilege and graft in his governments. Among his whims was the making of new capitals, for he was the founder of Williamsburg as well as of Annapolis. Despite the violent protests of the people of St. Mary's, he secured an act for the removal to the banks of the Severn, planned the town with streets radiating from State Circle, made shipping and trade zones and residential sections for the rich and others for artisans and laborers.

For several decades the place resembled more a mushroom western mining town than the center of culture which it later became, if we may credit Ebenezer Cook's description in his *Sot-Weed Factor.*

Up to Annapolis I went,
A city situate on a plain,
Where scarce a house will keep out rain.
The buildings framed of cypress rare
Resemble much our Southwark Fair.
But stranger here will scarcely meet
With market place, exchange or street.
And if the truth I must report,
'Tis not so large as Tottenham Court.

Twenty years later this picture no longer suited the facts, as William Parks, editor of the *Maryland Gazette*, pointed out with asperity. The sessions of the Assembly and of the courts brought a throng of prominent people, who crowded into the Three Blue Balls, or Reynold's Tavern, or the Ship Tavern, or visited friends, and contributed to the gaiety at dinners or dances at the governor's mansion. In the surrounding country were many prosperous planters who drove in to listen to the sermons of Reverend James Wootton in St. Ann's Church, or to witness a performance of *Hamlet* at the theater, or to join in the fun of the Tuesday Club or the Homony Club. During the winter months many moved in, bag and baggage, to stay until the coming of spring drove them back to their tobacco fields. They were joined by permanent residents of the little capital, government officials, many of them grown rich through large fees and the use of their influence to gain possession of great tracts of land to the west, Thomas Bladin, Benjamin Tasker, Daniel Dulaney, Edmund Jennings, Charles Carroll, and others.

We may judge of the refinement of Annapolis society from John Bernard's description of Carroll. "From the refinement of his manners a stranger would have surmised that he had passed all his days in the salons of Paris. He had all that suavity and softness in combination with dignity which bespeak the perfection of good taste. . . . Ease may be natural to a man, but elegance—the union of propriety with ease, must be acquired." Annapolis he thought should be termed the Bath of America.[1]

As in other colonial centers, the wealthy families looked to London for cultural leadership, and obediently, even eagerly, accepted the dictates of the imperial capital in literature, architecture, the theater, the artistic crafts, clothing, social customs. "The quick importation of fashions from the mother country is really astonishing," noted William Eddis in 1771. "I am almost inclined to believe that a new fashion is adopted earlier by the polished and affluent American than by many opulent persons in the great metropolis. . . . In short, very little difference is, in reality, observable in the manners of the wealthy colonist and the wealthy Briton."[2]

Eddis was surprised to find the pronunciation of the Marylanders accurate and elegant;[3] he was invited to attend balls where the English dances were gone through with as much propriety as though led by Beau Nash himself; at the local

[1] John Bernard, *Retrospections of America* (New York: Harper and Brothers, 1887), p. 85.

[2] William Eddis, *Letters from America* (London, 1792), pp. 112, 113.

[3] *Ibid.*, p. 59.

theater he enjoyed excellent performances; the residences of the wealthy vied with those of the English gentry; their gardens, though not large, were laid out with excellent taste; their dwellings were filled with English furniture, the tables laden with English silver.

Nonetheless, Maryland was not England; Annapolis was not London. Try as they would to conform in everything to English customs and styles, the group of wealthy planters and officials who made the little capital on the Severn a center of colonial culture could not escape the influence of America and of Maryland. Annapolis was the cultural center of eastern Maryland, and the culture of eastern Maryland was based upon the plantation system, with its staple tobacco crop and its slave labor. A Galloway and a Chew might wear English clothes, imitate English manners, read English books, but they remained Marylanders. The isolation of their life, the command of slaves, the attention to their crops, the marketing of their tobacco, their plantation economy so shaped their civilization that nothing could deprive it of its individuality. The culture of Annapolis was fundamentally American, Southern, Maryland, based on English traditions, and colored by the intimate contact with London.

In nothing is this more apparent than in education, for the Marylanders made a point of modeling their schools upon those of the mother country and of securing, where possible, Englishmen as teachers. In 1694, when a school named in honor of King William was established at Annapolis under an Act of Assembly, the Bishop of London sent over a master to teach "Latin, Greek, writing and the like." As an earnest of their interest in education, a number of leading men contributed to the erection of a school building, and Maryland's first "free school" entered upon a long and useful career.

In the private schools the master who could boast of an English education or of experience in teaching in England enjoyed a great advantage over his American trained rivals. When Thomas Lyttleton opened school in Annapolis in 1762, he was careful to announce that he had long been engaged in teaching "in and about London."[4] Even more impressive was William Kean's notice that he had been educated in Trinity College, Dublin, and "had been employed for many years in the most noted academies in England and Ireland."[5]

The course of study, also, in many respects followed English tradition. Kean, whose school was in Queen Anne's County, across the bay from Annapolis, emphasized "Latin, Greek, Hebrew, the Greek and Roman Histories and Antiquities," apparently devoting all his time to them, while an assistant, whom he announced as "a proper writing master," taught not only reading and writing, but "arithmetic–vulgar, decimal and duodecimal–geometry, planometry, trigonometry, surveying, gauging, Italian book-keeping, navigation and the proportions for horizontal dials."[6]

Most of the eastern Maryland schools specialized either in the ancient languages, or in English, or in mathematics. In Francis Callister's school the student was first grounded in arithmetic, and then carried on into roots, mensuration, gauging, trigonometry, surveying, navigation, astronomy, algebra, geometry, and Italian bookkeeping. The lad who completed this course was ready to take his place behind the desk of a countinghouse, or to begin his career on one of the vessels which plied between the Chesapeake Bay and the West Indies.[7] More suitable for the sons of the wealthy planters was the school at Lower Marlborough, where R. Philipson taught

[4] *Maryland Gazette*, January 28, 1762.
[5] *Ibid.*, January 17, 1765.
[6] *Ibid.*
[7] *Callister Papers*, p.339.

"after an entire new and most expeditious method, English, French, Latin, Greek, Hebrew, Print-hand, Roman and Italic," etc.[8] While their brothers were thus pouring over Tacitus or Cicero or navigation and bookkeeping, the girls were hard at work in Mary Salisbury's school or Mary Anne March's school at French, needlework, embroidering, or making tapestry.[9] To learn the latest steps in dancing, both boys and girls went to John Ormsby's dancing school, which, as he tells us, was patronized by "the principal gentlemen and ladies at Annapolis." Mr. Ormsby also gave instruction in fencing, which he describes as "the noble science of defence."[10]

It was a matter of grave concern to thoughtful Marylanders that for a college education they must send their sons to William and Mary, or to a northern institution, or across the Atlantic to Oxford or Cambridge. When the Academy of Philadelphia, later the University of Pennsylvania, opened its doors for instruction in 1751, it inserted an advertisement in the *Maryland Gazette*[11] pointing out the advantages it offered to Marylanders. It proved so convincing that a correspondent to the *Gazette*, who called himself Philo Marilandicus, could state that at least one hundred Marylanders were entered by 1754. The remedy, he thought, was to found a college at Annapolis, or possibly a college on each bank of the Chesapeake, at which Protestant youths could be educated better and more cheaply than in Philadelphia. For young Marylanders of the "Popish persuason," he admitted it would still be necessary to go to Europe for admission to the Catholic colleges of France, etc.[12]

What defects in his education remained after his return

[8] *Maryland Gazette*, December 13, 1759.
[9] *Ibid.*, February 21, 1754.
[10] *Ibid.*, August 4, 1757.
[11] *Ibid.*, February 27, 1751.
[12] *Ibid.*, March 21, 1754.

from college the youth could remedy by reading, for the bookshops in the circle surrounding the capitol were always full of the latest English works. It was characteristic of the gay, witty, pleasure-loving people of Annapolis that they should be the most avid readers of contemporary fiction. There was none of the suspicion of "frivolous writing" so common in Boston, and *Peregrine Pickle*, *Clarissa*, *Pamela*, *David Simple*, *Roderick Random*, *Tom Jones*, and *Amelia* were hardly off the press before they were read and discussed in the drawing rooms and clubs of Annapolis. Books of religion, though by no means excluded from the shelves of the Annapolis libraries, found there a far less prominent place than in many of the northern cities. Nor were the Marylanders such constant readers of the classics as the Virginians, and, though many a planter had his Cicero, Caesar, Horace, and Homer, they were to a large extent crowded out of the bookshops by works of travel, history, medicine, law, poetry, and fiction.

We gain an idea of the reading of the eastern Marylanders if we accompany William Rind to the wharf to unload the crates of books which have just come in on the *Betsy* and look over the titles, one by one, as he unpacks the volumes. A cosmopolitan lot they are, suited to the taste of the group of gentlemen and ladies who constituted Rind's customers: Smollett's *Compleat History of England*, Hume's *Essays*, Locke's *Essay Concerning Human Understanding*, Johnson's *Dictionary*, copies of *The Spectator*, *The Guardian*, *The Tatler*, and *The Rambler*, *Peregrine Pickle*, *David Simple*, and other novels, *Gil Blas*, Cato's *Letters*, Voltaire's *Louis XIV* and *The Life of Charles XII*, Pope's *Homer* and *Essay on Man*, Cicero's *Epistles*, Watt's *Logic*, *Life of Peter the Great*, *Paradise Lost*, Aesop's Fables, Ovid, Horace, etc.[13]

[13] *Ibid.*, July 8, 1760.

The good people of Annapolis seem to have been fond of borrowing books, and many a volume went from hand to hand until it was almost worn out. The owners found it in their hearts to forgive this abuse if they could get their books back, but this on occasion was difficult. One who had long suffered inserted a notice in the *Gazette* appealing to a borrower either to return the second volume of a certain work or else call and get the first volume. If he will look under the cover, he added, he will find the following inscription, "The wicked borrow and never return."[14] Henry Callister said he would be grateful to get his books back even though abused "according to custom." "I had not long ago returned me the *Art of Cookery* in such a pickle, that one would imagine it had been several times in the pot."[15]

We can surmise from his reading that the Marylander took his culture with a lightness that was foreign not only to the Bostonian or the Philadelphian, but even to the Virginian. To him the classics, the great English writers, the novelists were to be enjoyed as one enjoys a concert, or a game of cricket, or a bowl of punch. They were to be mixed in with laughter and song and conviviality. To the New Englander the reading of the classics was an act of devotion, to the Virginian a luxury, to the Marylander a glass of wine.

At the meetings of the Tuesday Club the reading of satirical and humorous poems and essays, interspersed with French, Latin, and Greek quotations, alternated with copious drafts from the punch bowl and the singing of convivial songs. In the mock history of the club, written by Dr. Alexander Hamilton and adorned with grotesque pictures, each member had a Latin name. Jonas Green, publisher of the *Maryland Gazette*,

[14] *Ibid.*, January 6, 1763.
[15] *Ibid.*, February 10, 1757.

was accorded the title of the Five P's—Poet, Printer, Punster, Purveyor, and Punch-Maker General. That the poetry was not of the best we judge from the "Pindaric Ode," addressed to the president of the club by the poet laureate:

Descend, ye muses from Parnassus hill,
And drop nepenthe in my raptur'd quill,
High, O High,
Let my tow'ring genius fly.

Whereas the Tuesday Club met in the residences of the members, the Homony Club assembled once a week at the Coffee House. Its purpose, too, was conviviality spiced with literature, and we may imagine the shouts of approval with which the members greeted the poem by J. Clapham upon accepting the post of poet laureate:

Oh still may mirth and freedom reign
Around this gaily social train;
And as the rolling year
Matures the plenteous crops of corn,
May homony our board adorn
And crown our suppers here.

Among the distinguished members of this club were William Paca, signer of the Declaration of Independence, Charles Willson Peale, the artist, and William Eddis, author of *Letters from America.*[16]

The literary effusions of the various clubs gave excellent practice for the more serious letters, editorials, and poems which appeared in the *Maryland Gazette.* Jonas Green, the editor, himself contributed many articles, while his friends account for others on the classics, philosophy, belles-lettres, history, etc. Typical was the plea of one Phil-Eleutheus for

[16] R. T. Haines Halsey, Social and Cultural Life of Maryland, MS.; W. B. Norris, *Annapolis* (Toronto: Carswell, 1925), pp. 61–71.

the study of history so that young and tender minds could "be taught to fall in love with amiable characters and habitually trained to act a parallel part themselves."[17] Compared with some of the gazettes in other colonial cities, Green's paper was newsy and readable, and the articles on political events are forceful, logical, and witty.

To such a society as that of Annapolis, with its dilettantes, its literary clubs, its dances and dinners, its jockey club, there was little opposition to the theater. It was with open arms that they welcomed the Hallams when they moved up from Virginia in 1752 and opened with *The Beggar's Opera* at the "New Theatre,"[18] and followed with *The Busy Body*, *The Beaux' Strategem*, *The Virgin Unmasked*, *The Recruiting Officer*, *The London Merchant*, *Damon and Phillida*, and other favorites.

With this brief taste of the stage the people of Annapolis had to be satisfied for eight years, when the company returned under the management of David Douglass. A momentous occasion it was when the "polite and numerous" audience crowded into the little theater to take their seats behind the governor and witness performances of *The Orphan* and *Lethe*. As Mrs. Hallam, her son Lewis, Mrs. Love, and others went through with their parts, they were greeted with prolonged applause, while there was great pride in the announcement that both the prologue and epilogue had been written by native Marylanders whose poetical works were greatly admired by "all encouragers of the liberal arts."[19]

Impatiently the little city waited for their favorites to pay them another visit, and in 1770, when the company stopped on its way to Virginia to present *Cymbeline* and one or two

[17] *Maryland Gazette*, June 7, 1745.
[18] *Ibid.*, June 18, 1752.
[19] *Ibid.*, March 6, 1760.

other plays, every effort was made to induce them to plan for a longer stay.[20] The actors obviously objected that the old theater, which was small and inconveniently situated, made a successful season impossible. Thereupon the governor set on foot a subscription to erect a new theater on "a commodious, if not an elegant plan," with each subscriber receiving tickets for two seasons. "The building is already in a state of forwardness and the day of opening is anxiously expected," wrote William Eddis in January 1771. It was too narrow for its length he thought, but the boxes were neatly decorated, the pit and gallery large, the stage well arranged, the scenes excellent.[21]

But it was the acting which excited Eddis's admiration. "When I bade farewell to England I little expected that my passion for the drama could have been gratified in any tolerable degree at a distance so remote from the great mart of genius. . . . My pleasure and my surprise were therefore excited in proportion in finding performers in this country equal at least to those who sustain the best of the first characters in your most celebrated provincial theatres."[22] No doubt Eddis shared in the enthusiasm for Sarah Hallam, "the sweetheart of colonial America," whose beauty and fine acting as Imogen spurred one Annapolis swain to sing her praises in verse:

> *When laid along thy grassy tomb,*
> *What pencil, say, can paint,*
> *Th' unlustrous, but expressive gloom*
> *Of thee, fair, sleeping saint!*

The same broad interest in cultural matters which displayed itself in the building of the theater explains why one of Amer-

[20] *Ibid.*, August 30, 1770.
[21] William Eddis, *op. cit.*, pp. 93–95.
[22] *Ibid.*

ica's earliest portrait painters made his home at Annapolis. It was in 1708 that Justus Engelhart Kühn set up his studio and started work on his canvases of the local gentry. Although his portraits of children, with their formal garden backgrounds and costumes in reds, browns, and blues, are not without merit, the stiffness of his figures and his inability to catch lifelike and revealing expressions expose his limited talent and his lack of adequate training. That he died a very poor man is explained in part by the inventory of his estate, which revealed that he had spent much time upon landscapes in an age when portraits alone brought an adequate return.

Perhaps it was Kühn's death which tempted Gustavus Hesselius to move from Philadelphia to Maryland, where he laid down an important milestone in the history of painting when he decorated St. Barnabas in Queen Anne Parish, "the first commission on record for a work of art for a public building in America." So satisfactory was his work that the vestry later engaged him "to draw the history of our blessed Saviour and the twelve apostles at the last supper . . . proportioned to the space over the altar piece." For this rather ambitious commission Hesselius received £17.

John Hesselius, son and pupil of Gustavus, who came to Annapolis in 1750, was a very inferior artist and is of interest chiefly as the early instructor of Charles Willson Peale, who paid him one of his best saddles for the privilege of watching while he painted a portrait. Peale, the son of a dissipated Englishman who had come to Maryland to escape punishment for embezzling funds, upon his father's death found himself a penniless boy, forced to apprentice himself to a saddler. Possessed of true American ingenuity, Peale, upon the termination of his service, turned his hand to anything which would bring in a shilling or two—upholstering, watchmaking, chair-making, silversmithing. When this jack of all trades turned his attention to painting, Governor Sharpe and ten members of the Maryland Council subscribed £83 to send him to London in the hope that he would add luster to the province. "The people here have a growing taste for the arts," wrote Peale himself, "and are becoming more and more fond of encouraging their progress."[23]

Peale was received with kindness by West and others in England and encouraged to remain to immerse himself in the neoclassicism then in vogue. But he disliked London, had no understanding of the theories or the brilliance of the English artists, and after two years returned to Annapolis. Yet his visit had inspired him to excel in his art, in his own literal American way. How fortunate this was we can realize from the fate which overtook Copley when he sacrificed his native genius in futile strivings for effects foreign to his nature and his early environment.

Peale could not rival Copley's power of looking behind the faces of the people he painted; his women, especially, being little more than pretty dolls. Yet, as James Thomas Flexner tells us, "the charm of his work was the charm of fresh vision. His colors, light greens and oranges and pinks, blended together with the warm innocence of spring flowers; he took a naïve delight in painting laces and the soft sheen of silks. And the poses of his figures, although more graceful than those typical of his American predecessors, have an underlying stiffness that gives them their particular flavor."[24] To Peale posterity will always be grateful for preserving the features of George Washington, who sat for him no less than fourteen times. It will acclaim him, also, as the embodiment of the early

[23] James T. Flexner, *op. cit.*, p. 189.
[24] *Ibid.*, p. 190.

American spirit, with all its optimism, versatility, simplicity, even crudeness, the spirit which laid the foundation of the America of today.

It is appropriate that Peale should have painted the portrait of William Buckland, for, as he himself dominated the field of painting at Annapolis, so Buckland stood out above all others in architecture. From its old frame the prepossessing face of a young man looks out at us, while on the table before him or in the background are the instruments and symbols of his art—pens, ink, books of architecture, plaster casts, the façade of a temple. Buckland it was who designed the Hammond House, the Chase house, and other beautiful residences, and impressed his ideas upon the architecture of all eastern Maryland.

Born in Oxford in 1734, he was apprenticed to an uncle in London, James Buckland, a member of the Carpenters and Joiners Guild and a bookseller. Young William not only learned from this uncle how to handle the saw and the hammer, but he had the opportunity of studying the books on architecture in his shop in Paternoster Row. In 1755, when Thomson Mason was in London, he engaged Buckland to come to Virginia to serve as technical adviser and master builder of Gunston Hall. This work completed, he came to Annapolis where he made his permanent home.[25]

His masterpiece was the Hammond House, which has been called the most beautiful Georgian building in America. As one views the two-story façade, the brick pilasters, the elaborate cornice, frieze, and architrave, the front door with its Corinthian columns, pediment, and arched transom, the evenly spaced windows capped with flat arches, the two wings connected with the main building by one-story links, one is impressed with the dignity, simplicity, and perfect proportions

[25] Richard T. H. Halsey, William Buckland, MS. lecture.

of the design. The Hammond House stamps Buckland as a master architect.

It is fortunate that so many of the Annapolis houses have escaped the destructive forces of time and fire and war, to testify to the good taste of the men who lived in them and perhaps had a hand in designing them. They could serve as the nucleus for a restoration that would be as interesting, though even more costly, than that of Williamsburg. They, with a number of near-by plantation residences, constitute a distinct type of architecture which we may properly call the Annapolis Georgian. It is characterized by a dignified central pavilion towering fifty feet or more above the ground, by balancing wings, by a high roof, by the absence of exterior shutters, by the flush trim and heavy muntins of the windows, by large, salmon-colored bricks with very narrow joints set in mortar made of sand and sea shells, by very high ceilings, and carved interior woodwork.[26]

In fact one wonders when he views the Hammond House, or Montpelier, at Laurel, or Tulip Hill, south of Annapolis, or the Chase house how the builders could adhere to the accepted rules of Georgian architecture and yet make them so typical of Maryland. It is not hard to discover the origin of the fundamental plan, for it occurs in almost every contemporary book of architecture; this lovely doorway we find in Kent's *Designs of Inigo Jones*, this circular window in James Gibbs's *A Book of Architecture*, this bit of exquisite carving in Johnson's *One Hundred and Fifty New Designs*. But the completed whole is unique, would be out of place anywhere else than eastern Maryland.

Although Buckland's was the master hand in the designing of these superb houses, he was neither the originator of the

[26] *Monograph Series*, XV, No. 5.

Annapolis style nor its sole exponent. An architectural style is a development, not an invention; and tradition, climate, building materials, as well as the taste and skill of builders and owners, combined to produce the Maryland Georgian. Among Buckland's books on architecture was one which was especially "designed as an agreeable entertainment for gentlemen and more particularly useful to all who make architecture and polite arts their study." There is ample evidence that Maryland gentlemen not only studied architecture for its cultural value, but to equip themselves for practical work. Although in most cases they collaborated with professional builders, their houses are monuments to their own good taste and architectural knowledge.

The interior carving was the work of master workmen, some of them real artists in wood. Henry Crouch was deemed by his contemporaries "as ingenious an artist at his business as any in the King's dominions." In addition to his work on the friezes, the architraves, the mantels of the Annapolis houses, he cut out separate human figures and even elaborate groups. In one of these we have Britannia, with a scepter in one hand and an olive branch in the other, on her right is the prostrate figure of France, while near by are clustered Envy struck dead by Jupiter, Ceres, Fame, and other figures. On the left of Britannia is Victory introducing Peace, Minerva, Fortitude, Neptune, and Mercury, while Time hovers above with his scythe and a pair of callipers with which he measures the globe.[27]

Crouch was not alone in his mastery of wood, for there were numerous excellent cabinetmakers in or near Annapolis who drove a skillful chisel. It is true that much of the beautiful furniture which adorned the drawing rooms and dining

[27] *Maryland Gazette*, January 7, 1762.

rooms of Tulip Hill, or the Paca house, or Homewood was made in England and brought to Maryland on the tobacco ships. One had only to step into the store of Stephen West to make a selection from his stock of imported "mahogany chairs and tables of all sizes, card tables, tea boards, elbow chairs, dressing tables, dressing glass and drawers, sconces," etc.[28] But near by were the workshops of John Anderson, Gamaliel Butler, William Hayes, Shaw and Chisholm, or Philip Williams, where furniture was made from the sawing and turning of the wood to the last stitch of the upholstering.[29]

Perhaps these men would have had difficulty in competing with the English craftsmen had they not enjoyed the advantage of an abundant supply of excellent wood at cheap prices. When Virginia or Maryland black walnut was sent to England to be made into chairs and tables which were sent back to the Chesapeake, the double freight tended to offset the cheaper cost of English manufacture. The Maryland cabinetmakers often used pine for a base and ash, oak, gum, and poplar for the framework. Black walnut was in constant demand, and in the later colonial days mahogany and cherry were used as veneers. When John Anderson died in 1759, his widow advertised for sale "a quantity of well-seasoned mahogany and walnut plank."[30]

Shaw and Chisholm not only made furniture themselves, but, paradoxically, catered to the wants of their competitors by carrying a large stock of cabinetmakers' tools—brass-mounted stocks; jack, trying, smoothing, and jointer planes; astricals; snipebill and oyes planes, etc.[31] The occasional advertising for journeymen cabinetmakers or the purchase of an

[28] *Ibid.*, June 25, 1752.
[29] *Ibid.*, July 11, 1754; April 4, 1754; September 22, 1747.
[30] *Ibid.*, May 17, 1759.
[31] *Ibid.*, May 6, 1773.

indentured worker trained to the craft indicate that the output of some of the shops was considerable. In others nothing more than repair work was done and the master, not finding work enough to employ all his time, turned his hand to other occupations. John Anderson sold candles and bacon; John Johnson kept a tavern in Lower Marlborough; Philip Williams occasionally interrupted his work to sharpen razors, scissors, and lancets; while Robert Harsnip's efforts to add to his income by building a gallows proved fatal when a beam fell and struck him on the head.[32]

Enough of the work of the Annapolis cabinetmakers has been identified to prove that it was excellent in design and skillfully executed. A secretary bearing the label of John Shaw displays great skill at inlaying, the oval design on the door with its acorns and leaves being the equal of the best done by the Hepplewhite school. The broken pediment and scroll work of another Shaw secretary show the influence of the Philadelphia school. In the last years of the colonial period many pieces of furniture found their way from the Quaker City to Annapolis, where they were greatly admired and no doubt imitated. In time, as more Annapolis furniture comes to light, we can evaluate better the ability of the local workers, but it is obvious that they constituted a group small in number and in workmanship inferior to that of the Philadelphia masters.

As we review the culture of colonial Annapolis, we find in it an elusive quality. Every well-to-do family proudly displayed its fine silverware in the corner cupboard or on the table, yet Annapolis produced no silversmiths comparable to Paul Revere or Philip Syng or Peter Van Dyck. There is abundant evidence that the Marylanders were fond of good

[32] *Ibid.*, May 6, 1762.

music and enjoyed a good opera or a private concert, but none won fame as a composer, or performer, or concert leader. They were insatiable readers, as the lists of the local bookstores abundantly prove, but rare indeed was it for one of them to write a volume of his own. They were interested in Franklin's experiments with electricity, but there was no distinguished Maryland scientist in the colonial period, no member of the Royal Academy. They early proclaimed their desire to give their sons the best possible education, but they neglected to found a college.

The Maryland aristocracy enjoyed culture, but they did not produce it. When they scribbled their verse for publication in the *Gazette* or to read before the gay group in the Tuesday Club or the Homony Club, it was with the spirit of the dilettante not with the burning zeal of the genius or the dogged persistence of the professional writer. They preferred Fielding and Richardson to Tillotson or Bunyan; Shakespeare's plays they enjoyed far more when presented on the stage than upon the printed page; they read and tried to imitate the meter and the mocking spirit of Pope rather than the stately lines of Milton.

The one physical monument to the refined, cultured life in the Maryland colonial capital which remains is the remarkable group of Georgian residences. None but men of taste, education, wealth could have built and lived in such houses. The dignified façades, the classic doors, the correct proportions, the mantels, the carving on cornices and pediments speak eloquently of courtly gentlemen and beautiful women, of gay dances and gayer parties, of discussions of the Indian troubles or the tobacco trade or the Stamp Act. In other words, these old buildings are not the crowning achievement of Annapolis, but evidence of it—the achievement of giving to the nation a group of farseeing, cultured, patriotic leaders. Had Annapolis no other claim to fame it would be enough that three of her sons—Charles Carroll, William Paca, and Samuel Chase—were signers of the Declaration of Independence.

"large small town"

THE MIND OF THE TOBACCO ARISTOCRAT

Williamsburg

THE restoration of colonial Williamsburg, which has aroused nationwide interest, is far more than the rebuilding of old houses; it is an attempt to depict in a vivid and fascinating way the civilization of which the town was the center. Williamsburg was never more than a village; it lacked the commercial importance of Boston or Philadelphia; unlike Charleston it was not a residential center for wealthy planters. It is true that on Sundays one might see the coaches of the parishioners of Bruton Parish waiting on the Palace Green or on the Duke of Gloucester Street while their owners listened to the sermons of Commissary Dawson, but most of the time Williamsburg was just a sleepy village in the midst of tobacco fields and woods.

It awoke to pulsing life several times a year, however. When the General Assembly held its sessions in the Capitol, every tavern was filled to overflowing with prominent persons from all parts of the province. The richly attired aristocrat from Gloucester or Charles City rubbed elbows with the Scotch-Irish frontiersman from Rockbridge or with the German settler from Shenandoah. Here were burgesses, members of the Council of State, planters with suits to plead in the General Court, yeomen with petitions to lay before the Assembly. There were stately balls in the governor's Palace, dinners at

Carter's Grove and other neighboring plantations, productions of *Hamlet* or *The Beggar's Opera* at the theater, every residence was overflowing with guests, there was drinking and singing around the bar in Raleigh Tavern.

Williamsburg was the social and cultural, as well as the political, capital of Virginia. It was the governor who set the style in matters of dress and decorum; and a new plant which found its way into his garden, or a new gown worn by his wife, or a new melody performed at his Palace concerts was sure to find favor with the planter aristocracy. It was Williamsburg which introduced Renaissance architecture into the colony and fixed the style which was to produce a Westover, a Brandon, an Elting Green. At Williamsburg, also, was the College of William and Mary, the intellectual center of the province, where young aristocrats—Carters, Nelsons, Pages—listened reverently to the lectures of Small and Wythe and other great teachers.

We must keep clearly in mind, however, that the intellectual life of the tobacco region was diffuse rather than centralized, that it was to be found not in any one town, but on a thousand plantations. George Washington enjoyed thoroughly his visits to Williamsburg, for they gave him the opportunity to meet old friends, to attend dinners and dances, to see a performance of *Othello*, but his chief interests were in Mount Vernon—in drawing plans for an addition to the mansion, in transplanting trees, in adding to his library, in purchasing prints of the paintings of Trumbull, or West, or Lorrain. The culture of Williamsburg was representative, not all-embracing; the town was the chief focal point in a life that was by its very nature centrifugal.

It was this very isolation which made it so difficult for the Virginians to build up an effective educational system. In

The governor's house set the style for the Colony

the seventeenth century, despite a few endowed schools here and there, the smaller planters found it necessary, after the day's work in the fields or on Sundays, themselves to instruct their children in reading and writing. With the accumulating of wealth in the eighteenth century schools became more numerous, and the children might be seen trudging along the roads or cutting through the woods to attend "old field" schools. Not infrequently ministers of the established church, glad to add to their meager salaries, opened schools, perhaps in the rectory, perhaps in a wing of some rich man's residence.

Many families solved the problem of education for their children by employing a tutor—possibly like Philip Fithian, a Princeton graduate, possibly a Scotsman just from Aberdeen, possibly the neighboring rector. The tutor was treated with respect by his employer, enjoying a pleasant chamber, eating with the family, and browsing at will in the library. When he had instilled into his youthful charges a fair knowledge of Latin, Greek, reading, arithmetic, and trigonometry, they were ready to enter college. For the average youth college meant William and Mary, for it stood alone south of Mason and Dixon's line and there was little thought of entering the Presbyterian college of Princeton or either of the New England colleges. Some well-to-do planters sent their sons to Oxford or Cambridge, but the expense was very heavy, the voyage dangerous, and the results not always satisfactory.

It was a brilliant group which William and Mary sent forth to play leading roles in the Revolution or in the creating of the nation—Thomas Jefferson, John Marshall, Peyton Randolph, Edmund Randolph, John Tyler, Sr., James Monroe, and others. To these men the professors were not only teachers, but friends and counselors. To Dr. William Small, Professor of Natural Philosophy and Mathematics, Jefferson

When the Burgesses was in session the town came to life.

paid a splendid tribute. "To his enlightened and affectionate guidance of my studies while in college I am indebted for everything. . . . He introduced . . . rational and elevated courses of study, and from an extraordinary conjunction of eloquence and logic, was enabled to communicate them to the students with great effect."[1]

The foundation of education in colonial Virginia was the classics. Jefferson expressed a universal view when he declared that "The Greeks and Romans have left us the present models which exist of fine composition, whether we examine them as works of reason, or style, or fancy. . . . To read the Latin and Greek authors in their original is a sublime luxury."[2] William Byrd II read Hebrew, Greek, and Latin fluently, and it was his established custom after rising in the morning and before saying his prayers to delve into Homer, or Josephus, or Lucian, or Cassius, or Herodian. Every accomplished gentleman was supposed to know his Homer and his Ovid, and in conversation was put to shame if he failed to recognize a quotation from either.

Having absorbed his share of the classics, the student usually went on to the study of law. Of those who wished to make the practice of law their profession, a few crossed the Atlantic to study at the Inns of Court in London; others attended Wythe's lectures at William and Mary. But every planter, especially the large planter, was supposed to know his Coke and his Blackstone. He had frequent occasion to make use of them as justice of the peace; they would certainly be needed in case he went to the House of Burgesses to represent his county; they would be indispensable if he attained the high honor of

[1] *Writings of Thomas Jefferson* (Washington, D. C.: Thomas Jefferson Memorial Association, 1905–1907), XIV, p. 231.

[2] *Ibid.*, XVIII, p. 146.

had one of the best theatres in Colonial Am.

a seat in the General Court; he could fall back upon them in a suit over a land patent or a long overdue debt to an English merchant.

Having received his diploma from the hands of President Horrocks, the youthful graduate of William and Mary returned to his father's home to take up the planter's life. But though the clearing of new fields, the putting out of crops, the erecting of barns and fences, the direction and care of slaves, the sale of tobacco and the purchase of goods from England took much of his time and energy, he did not neglect the things of the mind and soul. He could browse in his library, become an amateur architect, create a beautiful garden, indulge in music, and once or twice a year when he visited Williamsburg attend a production at the theater. The commonly accepted belief that the well-to-do Virginian was a "playboy," wasting his time and his inheritance in gambling, cockfighting, drinking, feasting, and dancing, is entirely erroneous. It is true that there was much extravagance, much gaiety, much dining and dancing, but there was also a keen interest in intellectual and cultural matters—literature, art, music, science, statecraft.

But intellectual life in Virginia was more receptive than creative. The planter might enjoy fine music, but he was seldom a composer; he might read Shakespeare and Milton, but he did not write plays or poetry; he might purchase fine paintings for his residence, but he was not a painter; he might study the works of Copernicus and Newton and Boyle, but he was not himself a scientist. Virginia in the colonial period produced no poet, save the writer of "Bacon's Epitaph, made by his Man," no novelist, no playwright, no great theologian, no artist, no sculptor, no outstanding architect. Yet there were hundreds who were interested in literature, art, architecture, music; might themselves be amateur writers, architects, musicians.

Yet the Virginians were by no means mere intellectual drones. The chief literary output is unpublished, consisting as it does of the great mass of letters, reports, and other official documents reposing in the Public Record Office in London, and, in this country, diaries, private journals, and letters preserved in private and public libraries. When we read these papers we discover that Reverend James Blair was a master of convincing argument; that Sir Francis Nicholson is almost unmatched in sarcastic invective; that Sir William Berkeley has the art of expressing himself vigorously in pithy, biting sentences; that Nathaniel Bacon, the patriot, was an orator of no mean ability. *The Present State of Virginia*, by Hartwell, Blair, and Chilton, recently published by the Department of Research and Record of Colonial Williamsburg, Inc., is an informative document, written in a clear and interesting style.[3] The correspondence of leading statesmen—Washington, Mason, Jefferson, Pendleton, Peyton Randolph, and others—in itself constitutes a considerable body of fine literature.

Nor was colonial Virginia without its published works. Robert Beverley, Hugh Jones, and William Stith wrote histories of Virginia which have considerable merit and were widely read. At Williamsburg William Rind, or William Hunter or Purdie and Dixon, or William Parks kept their presses busy turning out the *Virginia Gazette*, now so indispensable for the student of colonial life. This sheet, which embraced the usual four pages, besides its four or five columns devoted to rehashed European news, its notices of runaway slaves or lost horses, or plantations for sale, or the arrival of

[3] Hunter D. Farish, editor.

a cargo of European goods, not infrequently published poetical efforts dilating on the charms of Myrtilla or of Florella, or reprinted articles from *The Spectator* or *The Rambler*. When the paper had been turned off, the printers occupied themselves until the next issue with works of various kinds—a sermon delivered before the General Assembly by William Stith,[4] a "Poem on Winter" printed for the benefit of a poor child,[5] a plan for an academy, Tucker's poem "The Bermudian,"[6] John Bland's sermon *The Crisis*, the *Whole Body of Laws*, pamphlets denouncing the Stamp Act.[7]

The genius of the people expressed itself, however, not so much in literature as in statecraft. They became students of politics and government, examined the workings of the Swiss Republic and the ancient democracies, poured over Locke and Montesquieu, discussed the principles of human rights at the dinner table or while riding to church or to court. When Jefferson founded the University of Virginia it was necessary for him to send abroad for his professors of ancient languages, modern languages, and mathematics, but for his professors of law and of political economy he turned to Francis W. Gilmer, George Tucker, John Tayloe Lomax, John A. G. Davis, graduates of William and Mary all of them.[8] It was not by chance that George Mason wrote the Virginia Bill of Rights, that Thomas Jefferson wrote the Declaration of Independence, that James Madison became the Father of the Constitution, that Patrick Henry sounded the "fire bell of the Revolution." These men were raised in an atmosphere of political activity

[4] *Virginia Gazette*, March 20, 1752.
[5] *Ibid*., February 16, 1769.
[6] *Ibid*., June 2, 1774.
[7] *Ibid*., August 25, 1774.
[8] J. B. Henneman, "Historic Elements in Virginia Education, etc.," Virginia Historical Society *Proceedings*, 1891.

and political thought, were outstanding representatives of a race of statesmen and political philosophers.

The planter's joy and pride was his library. When his day's visit to the tobacco fields was over, or he had given his instructions to the overseers or had completed plans for a new orchard or a tobacco house, he retreated to the library to unlock one of the bookcases, select a volume, and lose himself in its pages. If, like Jefferson and Byrd, he delighted in the classics, he could make his selection from Caesar, Cicero, Ovid, Horace, Livy, Virgil, Aristotle, Homer, Plutarch, Sallust, and many others. If he were interested in religious literature, he had before him a *Brief Treatise on the Testaments*, *The Christian Sacrifice*, *The Whole Duty of Man*, etc. In the English classics he had the works of Shakespeare, Milton, Dryden, Swift, Pope, Bacon, or the recent works of fiction—*Tom Jones*, *The Vicar of Wakefield*, *Tristram Shandy*, *Roderick Random*, *Humphrey Clinker*, *Peregrine Pickle*. If he wished to turn to more practical things he could dig into James Gibbs's *A Book of Architecture*, or the *Complete Farmer*, or *The Surgeon's Mate*, or *The Country Justice*.

When he rode into Williamsburg to attend a meeting of the Assembly, his time was not so taken up with business that he would not wander into Dixon and Hunter's bookstore to look over their latest importations and to fill gaps in his own collection. There he found Chamber's *Dictionary of Arts and Sciences*, *Priestley on Electricity*, Ferguson's *Astronomy*, Pope's *Works* in five volumes, Young's *Experimental Agriculture*, Bunyan's *Pilgrim's Progress*, a *History of Paraguay*, Hume's *Essays*, *The Antiquities of Rome*, Lord Bacon's *Letters*, *The History of Scotland*, Shakespeare's *Works*, Shaw's *Practice of Physic*, Shaw's *Chemical Lectures*, *Don Quixote*, Aesop's Fables, Fielding's *Works*, *Gil Blas*, *Gulliver's Travels*,

Locke's *Thoughts Concerning Education*, and many more.[9] The chances were that when he returned to his plantation he had several volumes tucked away in his saddlebags and others set aside for delivery by wagon or river boat.

The Virginia private libraries were not only varied in content but large in size. William Byrd II gathered around him at Westover nearly four thousand volumes, George Washington owned nine hundred and three, Robert Carter had a thousand and sixty-six at Nomini Hall and five hundred at his Williamsburg residence. In the days when books were costly such large collections could be afforded only by the wealthiest, while the small planters and even the moderately well-to-do had to content themselves with from ten to a hundred volumes. The clergy, because of their rather meager incomes, could not afford the luxury of a large library, and many of them wrote to the Bishop of London or the Society for the Propagation of the Gospel for a few urgently needed works. Reverend James Maury's collection of four hundred volumes and forty-four pamphlets was exceptional.[10]

The culture of the Virginia planters lives again in our minds when we visit one of the old mansions on the James or the Potomac to wander through the spacious rooms or stroll along the box-lined paths of the garden. Here is the dining hall, where bounteous feasts were spread before the guests, here the reception room, the scene of dignified dances and gay assemblies, here the library, here the schoolroom, here the office, where the owner kept his accounts and transacted business with his overseers. The house itself reflects his taste in architecture, the furniture and silver in artistic craftsmanship, the library his literary and scientific interests, the garden his

[9] *Virginia Gazette*, November 25, 1775.

[10] *Virginia Magazine*, VII, p. 302.

love of flowers and landscaping, perhaps his interest in botany. We cannot know George Washington unless we know Mount Vernon; we are unacquainted with Thomas Jefferson unless we know Monticello; Westover is the very expression of William Byrd II.

In architecture, as in so many other things, the planters turned to England for guidance. The seventeenth-century Virginia cottage is an East Anglian house modified by conditions in the colony—by the climate, building materials, the rural life, the high cost of labor. Bacon's Castle, which seems to have been a typical residence of the well-to-do planter in Sir William Berkeley's day, is a Tudor country house. When Renaissance architecture, under the leadership of Inigo Jones and Sir Christopher Wren, became the vogue in England, it was inevitable that it would spread to the Chesapeake Bay region. The Wren Building at William and Mary, the Capitol, and the Palace definitely committed Virginia to the new style, and the wealthy planters followed suit with Westover, Carter's Grove, Elting Green, Brandon, and scores of other beautiful Georgian residences.

But these houses, within the restrictions set by the accepted style, expressed the individual tastes and the architectural ideas of the planters who built them. There were professional architects in Virginia, in some cases brought all the way from England to design certain houses, but the usual procedure was for the owner to employ a builder, designated "carpenter," and collaborate with him in drawing up the plans and specifications. Thomas Jefferson took unending delight in creating his beloved Monticello, and made no less than four separate plans before settling upon the final design and beginning construction. Mount Vernon as it stands today is the work of George Washington, for it was he who changed the place from a simple Virginia cottage into a pretentious mansion by adding a story, building wings to right and left, putting up a portico, capping the whole with a cupola. Even amid the activities and perils of the French and Indian War he found time to think of the work going on at the house on the Potomac and write to England for "a marble chimney piece," for papier-mâché for the ceilings, for 250 panes of window glass, "a dozen fashionable locks," and "fashionable hinges."[11]

Styles in building were fixed partly by the visits of Virginians to England, partly by English architects in the colony, partly by the study of English books of architecture. There is reason to believe, also, that Henry Cary, builder of the Capitol at Williamsburg, and other native Virginians went to England to study architecture. In most cases we may assume that the owner and the "carpenter," seated at a table, spread out before them James Gibbs's *A Book of Architecture*, Isaac Ware's *A Complete Body of Architecture*, Batty Langley's *City and Country Builder's and Workman's Treasury of Designs*, and other similar books to select a plan most suited to their needs. This they altered to meet conditions in Virginia, adding to or subtracting from the dimensions, removing the kitchen to a wing or an outhouse, replacing the marble of windows and doors with brick. For details, exterior as well as interior, they might make one selection from Gibbs, another from Ware, still another from Swan. The Palladian windows in the wings of Mount Vernon, Washington took almost unchanged from Batty Langley.

The residence completed, the planter turned to the laying out and planting of his garden. Here too he was influenced by English styles and English books, perhaps selecting a plan from

[11] T. H. Ormsbee, "Clear Facts About Old Glass," *House Beautiful*, February 1934.

The Compleat Gardener, or from *The Retired Gardener*, or from *Rapin on Gardening*.[12] These books showed only the formal design, drawn chiefly from France, with its box-lined walks, brick stairs, corner summerhouses, mazes, ornamental gates, colorful flower beds, and lines of fruit trees. The planter imported English shrubs, flowers, and trees and subjected them to the test of actual trial in the Virginia climate. Some, like the box, flourished, others languished in the summer's heat or the relative dryness. At Ash Grove one finds in the old terraced garden the remnants of flowers which date back to the days of the Fairfaxes—snowballs, daffodils, peonies, Madonna lilies, fleur-de-lis, glorious roses, one a huge single-blossom rose of deep pink, with long stems, ornamental leaf, and fine long buds, another the Lancaster and York rose, its petals of delicate pink and white.[13]

The Palace garden, now beautifully restored by Colonial Williamsburg, Inc., was clearly patterned upon the late seventeenth-century English garden, perhaps that of Eaton Hall, Shropshire, which it closely resembled. Today thousands of visitors wander over its walks lined with superb tree box, or descend the terraces of the Falling Garden to the canal and the fishpond, or admire the Fruit and Vine Garden, or linger in the Box Garden or the Ball-Room Garden to enjoy the profusion of beautiful flowers. It was this fine creation which set the style in colonial Virginia, for every wealthy planter who dined with the governor or attended a dance in the ballroom returned home with the determination to imitate its beauties. The gardens at Westover, Stratford, and elsewhere, though less extensive than that at Williamsburg, are clearly patterned after it.

[12] J. A. Bassett, ed., *The Writings of Col. Wm. Byrd* (New York: Doubleday, Page and Company, 1901), pp. 422, 425.

[13] *William and Mary Quarterly*, Series Two, VII, p. 88.

The wealthy Virginian prided himself upon the portraits which adorned his walls, painted by Sir Godfrey Kneller, or Sir Peter Lely, or Thomas Sully, or the wandering artists Charles Bridges and John Wollaston. If he happened to be in England on business, he often availed himself of the opportunity to have his portrait painted by one of the popular artists of the day, otherwise he had to avail himself of men of less ability who came to America seeking to earn a living with the brush. Wollaston traversed the colony, painting George Washington's mother, Thomas Mann Randolph, Speaker John Robinson, and others. Charles Bridges has left us portraits of Lucy Park Byrd, Colonel Edward Hill, Mann Page II, Colonel Matthew Page, Mrs. Lewis Burwell, etc.[14]

The walls of the apartments of Westover were hung with dozens of fine paintings, portraits, and engravings. Here was a painting by Titian, there one by Rubens, there an engraving showing the offering of Abraham, here hung portraits of the Duchess of Montaigne, here Evelyn Byrd, here John Tayloe, here Charles Carter, here Colonel Peter Randolph and Mrs. Randolph, here Charles Boyle, Earl of Orrery, here Sir Wilfried Lawson, here the Marquis of Halifax, here the Duke of Argyle, here Sir Robert Southall, here in the hallway a full-length portrait of William Byrd III, in the lower southeast room a painting of William Byrd II, there Lady Betty Cromwell.[15] Philip Fithian tells us that at Mount Airy the mansion was "ornamented with various paintings and rich pictures." Washington surrounded himself with prints of famous paintings—*The Battle of Bunker Hill*, *The Thunder Storm*, Lorrain's *Evening*, Wooton's *The Death of the Fox*, etc.

For his furniture the planter, as in so many other things, turned to England. The ships which left the Chesapeake Bay

[14] *Virginia Magazine*, IX, pp. 236, 237.
[15] *Ibid.*, VI, pp. 346–351.

each year, filled to the gunwales with tobacco hogsheads, returned with a far less bulky cargo of English manufactured goods, so that space was available even for such unwieldy articles as tables, beds, secretaries, and chairs. Thus the English visitor to Virginia might be surprised to find at Nomini Hall or Tuckahoe or Carter's Grove duplicates of the furniture in his own house in London. Upon inquiry he would discover that it had been fashioned perhaps by the same cabinetmaker, possibly in the shop of Chippendale himself. It was this which prevented the development of a group of cabinetmakers at Williamsburg comparable to the Philadelphia masters.

Yet there were cabinetmakers in the tiny Virginia capital whose workmanship seems to have been of a high order. Had not Benjamin Bucktrout been skilled in his trade, Robert Carter of Nomini Hall would not have ordered from him "eight mahogany chairs stuffed with black leather" and eight mahogany "elbow chairs."[16] Bucktrout proudly announced in the *Gazette* that he was "from London," and that he did "all kinds of cabinet-work, plain or ornamental."[17] Among the other Williamsburg cabinetmakers were Matthew Moody, Jr., Honey and Horrocks, who made it clear that in addition to repair work they made "cabinets, tables, etc.," Anthony Hay, noted as the proprietor of the Raleigh Tavern, James Kidd, etc.

It is to be hoped that enough of the work of these men may some day be identified to make it possible to judge of its character. Much was no doubt destroyed during the Revolution and the War Between the States, hundreds of pieces wore out with decades of use and were discarded, industrious housewives have scrubbed the maker's labels from almost all that

[16] Robert Carter Account Books, 1759–79, June 14, 1774.

[17] *Virginia Gazette*, July 25, 1766.

remains, so that it is impossible to say that this table was done by Bucktrout, this cabinet by Honey and Horrocks. We know, however, that the local cabinetmakers followed the prevailing English styles, that many of them had at hand English books of design, and that some came to Williamsburg directly from English shops. We have reason to think, then, that they were inferior to the northern craftsmen in the bulk of their output rather than in the quality of their work.

Nor was Williamsburg without its goldsmiths and silversmiths who turned out spoons, candlesticks, ladles, and teapots for the sideboards of the neighboring planters. William Waddell advertised that he had for sale "table and tea spoons, sugar tongs," tureen and punch ladles, mourning rings, etc. "Old gold and silver will be taken at the highest price in exchange for new work," he added, "or worked up in any taste the owner chooses."[18] We have no way of determining the skill and artistry of the men who worked under the "Sign of the Dial, Harp and Crown," or the "Sign of the Golden Ball," but there is no reason to think that it was inferior to that of the English or northern smiths.

Williamsburg has the honor of being the birthplace of the American stage, for there, on the green near the Palace, two and a quarter centuries ago, was erected the first theater. It was one William Levingston, in partnership with Charles and Mary Stagg, dancing teachers newly arrived from London, who erected the little building and staged a series of "comedies, drolls and other kinds of stage plays." The partners were to share the expenses of "clothes, music and other necessaries" and agreed to send to England for actors and musicians. That there was no serious opposition to the stage in Virginia is shown by the list of distinguished patrons, among them gover-

[18] *Ibid.*, (Parke), September 17, 1767.

nors, members of the Council of State, burgesses, and wealthy planters.

This little theater must have accomplished much to fix the dramatic taste of the Virginians and interest them in the stage. But that they were occasionally more interested in each other than in the performance, we gather from a letter in the *Virginia Gazette* of October 22, 1736, "Whereas a gentleman who towards the latter end of summer usually wore a blue gamlet coat lined with red and trimmed with silver, a silver laced hat and a turpee wig has often been observed by his amoret to look very languishingly at her . . . and particularly one night during the last session of Assembly, at the theatre, the said gentleman ogled her in such manner as showed him to be very far gone. The said amoret desires the gentleman to take the first opportunity that offers to explain himself on that subject." We are not informed of the outcome of this budding romance.

In 1751 the play-loving Virginians united to erect a crude theater back of the Capitol, handing in their subscriptions to Alexander Finnie, the genial host of the Raleigh Tavern. A year later it was taken over by a group of actors who arrived in the *Charming Sally* and converted it into "a regular theater fit for the reception of ladies and gentlemen and the execution" of the best performances. The coming of Lewis Hallam, his wife, their little son, Lewis, Jr., Mr. Rigby, and others of this company marks an epoch in the history of the American stage, and the amateurish attempts of local actors gave way to professional presentations of a high order. So it was a momentous occasion when the Hallams announced that they would begin "with a play call'd the *Merchant of Venice* (written by Shakespeare) and a farce, call'd *The Anatomist* or *Sham Doctor*. The ladies are desired to give timely notice to Mr. Hallam, at Mr. Fisher's, for their places in the boxes, and on the day of performance to send their servants early to keep them in order to prevent trouble and disappointment."

Now followed plays by Shakespeare, Congreve, Garrick, Gay, and others in quick succession. With the opening of the sessions of the General Court the theater was crowded to overflowing night after night and some performances brought in as much as £300. The repertoire seems to have been almost inexhaustible, for there was a different performance each night, with brief farces and comedies between acts. So the planters and their wives grieved at the sorrows of *Romeo and Juliet*, or pitied the unfortunate *Othello*, or laughed at comedies which would have shocked even the sophisticated audiences of today.

Although the Virginians could indulge their taste for the theater only when they visited Williamsburg, there was no such restriction upon the enjoyment of good music. Many of the planters themselves played musical instruments, employed teachers to instruct their daughters on the spinet or the pianoforte, sent out for a small orchestra whenever they held a ball, joined in the singing at church, perhaps organized a local musical club. One likes to think of those evenings at the Palace when the youthful Jefferson joined with Governor Fauquier and his guests in a musical feast. And it is most appropriate that today, in the restored mansion, there are performances upon instruments popular in colonial days of music selected from Jefferson's library.

The violin was popular, and it was in constant use for the playing of jigs at a country dance, or as part of the orchestra at the theater or for a ball at Mount Airy or Lee Hall or Westover, or for a concert devoted to the works of the masters. But other instruments were also common—spinets, organs, harpsichords, French horns, German flutes, common flutes, trumpets, hautboys, guitars, harmonicas. Robert Carter had at Nomini Hall a harpsichord, pianoforte, harmonica, guitar, and several German flutes, and at his Williamsburg residence an organ.[19] Fithian tells us that "law and music" were the Colonel's main studies, "the latter his darling amusement," in which he had made advances in theory and practice.[20]

The taste in music seems to have been good. Had we entered the bookstore of Hunter and Dixon to thumb through the sheet music on sale, we would have found Stamitz's *Orchestral Trios* and selections from Richter, Campioni, Schwindl, and others. Cuthbert Ogle, the music teacher, was devoted to Handel, and counted in his music cabinet ten books of his songs, some of his oratorios, and his *Apollo's Feast*. The first organ in the South was installed in Bruton Church in 1752 with Peter Pelham, Jr., as the organist, and often on summer evenings the villagers could hear through the open door the strains of Handel's masterpieces.[21]

One seldom associates the Virginia planter with the study of science, yet there were many who pursued it, not only through the reading of books but by actual experiment. There was nothing unusual in the conversation at Nomini Hall, which Fithian describes, when Colonel Carter began a discussion of philosophy, which turned to "eclipses, the manner of reviewing them, thence to telescopes and the information which they afford us of the solar system, whether the planets be actually inhabited, etc."[22] John Page, of Rosewell, not only made a study of astronomy, but calculated a total eclipse of

[19] Philip Vickers Fithian, *Journal and Letters*, edited by Robert G. Albion and Leonidas Dodson (Princeton, N. J.: Princeton University Press, 1934), p. 59.

[20] *Ibid.*, p. 83.

[21] *William and Mary Quarterly*, XVI, p. 179.

[22] Philip Vickers Fithian, *op. cit.*, p. 176.

the sun and published his results in the local almanac. Landon Carter experimented with Sicilian wheat on his plantation in Richmond County, and published a treatise on the wheat weavil. William Byrd II was a botanist of no mean ability.

This scientific trend found expression on the eve of the Revolution in the founding of the Society for the Advancement of Useful Knowledge, under the patronage of the scholarly governor, Francis Fauquier. John Clayton, author of *Flora Virginica*, was elected president; John Page, vice-president; Reverend Samuel Henley, Professor of Moral Philosophy at William and Mary, secretary; St. George Tucker, assistant secretary; and David Jameson, treasurer.[23] Formed in imitation of the Royal Society, it devoted itself to the stimulation of the arts, manufactures, and science.[24]

Foremost among Virginia scientists was John Clayton, who came to America in 1705 and throughout his long career devoted every spare moment to the flora of the colony. His botanical garden at "Windsor" was filled with rare plants from almost every county in Virginia from the Blue Ridge to the Chesapeake. Clayton corresponded regularly with Gronovius and Linnaeus, and left at his death two manuscript volumes which were destroyed during the Revolution. Fortunately his *Flora Virginica* was published by Professor Gronovius and so escaped a similar fate.[25]

Distinguished in England as well as America was John Banister, minister in the parish of Appomattox. Believing with Samuel Stanhope Smith that scientific investigation was an act of devotion to the Creator, this country parson entered en-

[23] *Virginia Gazette* (Purdie and Dixon) May 13, 1773.
[24] *William and Mary Quarterly*, V, pp. 200, 201.
[25] John W. Campbell, *History of Virginia* (Petersburg, Va., 1813), pp. 182–183.

thusiastically upon a study of Virginia fauna and flora. His catalogue of plants, published in John Ray's *Historia Plantarum*, and his "Insects of Virginia," "Curiosities in Virginia," "On Several Sorts of Snails," and "Description of the Snake Root," published in the *Philosophical Transactions* of the Royal Society, give testimony to his ability.[26]

While Clayton was taking time from his duties as clerk of Gloucester County to hunt out rare plants and Banister was laying aside the Bible for a study of insects or of snake root, Dr. John Mitchell found opportunity when not busy with his patients to devote himself to botany, electricity, agriculture, and cartography. Intense indeed must have been the intellectual curiosity of a country physician who could publish a paper describing thirty species of plants, study yellow-fever epidemics, inquire into the causes of human coloring, investigate "the force of electrical cohesion," publish a treatise on agriculture, prepare a map of British America.

The Virginia gentleman was not the godless person he has often been represented, who took his religion lightly and went to church not because he was interested in the future of his soul, but merely to loiter outside to gossip with friends and relatives. It is true that he saw no harm in amusements which shocked the puritanical Philip Fithian—dancing, cockfighting, horse racing, dice, cards—but his library was stocked with religious books, he said his prayers devoutly, he listened reverently to the sermons of a Blair or a Dawson. "I read a sermon of Dr. Tillotson's which affected me very much and made me shed some tears of repentance," wrote William Byrd in his *Secret Diary* in May 1710. "About 11 o'clock we went to church and took possession of the pew which the vestry gave us," he wrote in December 1710. "We began to give in to the

[26] American Antiquarian Society, *Proceedings*, XXV, p. 358.

new way of singing Psalms. . . . In the afternoon my wife and I took a walk about the plantation. In the evening I read a sermon and wrote a letter. . . . I said my prayers and had good health, good thoughts and good humor, thank God Almighty." Such was a typical Sunday in the life of this wealthy and sophisticated Virginian.[27]

Although Williamsburg seldom resounded to the noise of contending theologians, it had its able divines, whose sermons compared favorably with those of the most earnest and erudite of Calvinists. Commissary James Blair, who for so many years played a leading political as well as religious role in the life of the colony, was a farsighted leader, a great educator, an eloquent preacher. Thomas Dawson, James Horrocks, Bartholomew Yates, and many others were learned and pious ministers and able theologians.

It was in the seclusion of their private libraries that the Virginians, turning to the standard works on religion, read and meditated on religious problems and prayed for enlightenment and guidance. Robert Carter, in his library at Nomini Hall, had many volumes on religion– *Hammond on the New Testament*, the *Works of Erasmus*, *Atterbury's Sermons*, Ray's *Wisdom of God*, *The Religious Philosopher*, *Defense of Christian Revelations*, *A Gentleman's Religion*, etc. Carter was a man of intense religious conviction, and, after a careful examination of the beliefs of the Deists which were affecting some of his friends, turned his back upon them. "Many good natured Deists will perish and my heart is wounded with sad apprehension of it," he wrote. In 1778 this aristocrat, who had been reared in the Anglican Church, as had his father and grandfather before him, went over to the Baptists.

[27] Louis B. Wright and Marion Tinling, *The Secret Diary of William Byrd of Westover* (Richmond, Va.: The Dietz Press, 1941), p. 276.

Could those who have made the accusation of cultural sterility against the Virginia planters have visited Williamsburg during the session of the Assembly they would have been forced to concede their error. They would have seen much, it is true, to convince them of the common love of gaiety—elegant dinners, stately dances, horse races, costly attire, some gambling, some excessive drinking. But in charming old Bruton Church they could have listened to an inspiring sermon by Commissary Blair; at the theater near the Capitol they could have crowded in to see a production of *Hamlet* or *Othello;* they could have stopped in at the "Sign of the Golden Ball" to see the silversmith at work on his beakers or porringers; have dallied at Bucktrout's cabinetmaking shop while the skilled workman turned out his chairs and tables; at the Palace they would have admired the superb gardens and wondered at the good taste which created them; entering the Palace itself the strains of classic music performed by skilled musicians might have greeted their ears; on the walls of the reception rooms or in the hallway they might have seen portraits painted by the ablest artists of the period; at the Capitol they would have heard some eloquent orator holding forth before the House of Burgesses in one room, while in another a distinguished advocate pleaded a case before the General Court. When at last they turned their backs upon the little village, with its varied and intensely interesting life, they would have been convinced that it was far indeed from meriting the charge of intellectual apathy.

RICE, INDIGO, AND ELEGANCE

Charleston

MORE than any other city in colonial America, Charleston was the product of the melting pot. Boston, Philadelphia, Annapolis, and Williamsburg were English from the first and their cultural development was not deeply affected by other peoples. The story of New York was the story of Dutch civilization yielding slowly to English civilization. But Charleston was peopled by groups from England, the West Indies, and continental Europe, with different customs, traditions, religions, arts, and even languages. A full century passed after the founding of the town before the merging of these diverse cultures, together with the influence upon them of English culture and of local conditions, produced a new and unique civilization, the civilization of the Carolina low country.

To this day Charleston retains much of its West Indian flavor and visitors from the North note with interest that the stuccoed houses, the iron balconies, the two- or three-tiered piazzas, the tiled roofs are more in the style of Barbados or Jamaica than of other American cities. And here and there one finds a gable end whose curving ends suggest the influence of Holland, or a red pantiled roof in the manner of southern France, while the dignified old Georgian mansions speak eloquently of the influence of England. The Charlestonian of the eighteenth century was unique in that one grandparent might have been born in England, another in France, another in Barbados, and the fourth in Holland.

Charleston differed from other cities, also, in that its culture was shaped jointly by merchants and planters. It was as though in Virginia Williamsburg had been transplanted to the banks of the Elizabeth, where Carters and Ludwells intermarried with Jamiesons or McIntoshes. It was partly the fear of sickness in the marshy rice plantations that drove many families to Charleston, partly the gay social life of the southern metropolis, with its dinners, balls, races, plays, and concerts. On the quaint old streets of the city in colonial days this house belonged to the owner of a warehouse and a brig or two, the next to a rice and indigo planter whose wide acres were located on the Ashley or the Cooper, the next to a man who was both merchant and planter and divided his time between his countinghouse and his rice fields. In fact, many Charleston merchants, having acquired a small fortune in trade, invested part of it in land, while many planters found it profitable to become partners in mercantile ventures.

A glance at the busy harbor would have convinced us of the importance to Charleston of its commerce. Here we see slips, brigs, snows, and schooners taking on their cargoes of indigo and rice at the wharves, or heading out to sea for the West Indies, or England, or New England, or Lisbon. There, coming in past Sullivan Island, or warping in at the Battery, are vessels from London or Cowes laden with manufactured goods for the colony—clothing, cloth, shoes, gloves, hats, axes, firearms, silverware, furniture, medicines. In 1767 there went out from Charleston no less than 110,072 barrels of rice, of which 64,340 went to English ports and 17,385 to the West Indies.

This trade was handled in part by British merchants, but it

brought wealth also to native Charlestonians, whose warehouses lined the Batteries and whose handsome residences graced Tradd or Lower Meeting Streets. Of these perhaps the wealthiest was Gabriel Manigault, philanthropist, provincial treasurer, a member of the Commons, benefactor of the Library Society, large land and slave holder. He died in 1781 leaving an estate estimated at $845,000.[1] Other prominent merchants were Isaac Mazÿck, Henry Laurens, Benjamin Smith, Andrew Rutledge, Miles Brewton, and Robert Pringle.

It was rice which brought wealth to the Carolina low country and rice which made society aristocratic rather than democratic. Since the culture of this crop required a considerable outlay of capital for the throwing up of levees, the construction of reservoirs and water gates, as well as for the purchase of slaves, the poor farmer found it difficult to participate in it. So the banks of the Ashley and the Cooper were lined with one rich plantation after another, each boasting of its mansion, its beautiful garden, and its scores of slaves. And each boasted, also, of its "pettiaugers" or great canoes which brought the planter's crop to Charleston and, with the approach of the "sickly season," carried his family to their city residence.

Charleston, then, became the center of a refined society which delighted in laying out its wealth in beautiful houses, stately balls, in luxurious gardens, in costly dinners, in musical entertainments, in the theater, in portraits, in literary clubs, in fine furniture and silver. Drawing their inspiration from the English squires, the Charlestonians vied with them in all the amenities of life and the graces of the cultured gentleman. Although wealth was the basis of this refined society, in time wealth alone was not sufficient to admit one to it. The "new

[1] Edward McCrady, *The History of South Carolina under the Royal Government* (New York: The Macmillan Company, 1899), pp. 402–404.

gentleman or rather half gentleman" who had acquired money but no culture was scorned as an upstart, a ridiculous "mulatto gentleman" as it were.[2]

Charleston culture was the product of three forces—the heterogeneous origins of its people, the influence of the mother country, and the molding effect of local conditions in the city and surrounding country.

In nothing is this more apparent than in architecture. The single house, so typical of early Charleston architecture, which presents the narrow end to the street, with the main door in the center of the long side, seems to have been introduced by the Dutch. But when one views the stuccoed walls, the picturesque pantiles of the roof, the iron balcony, the Huguenot districts of France come instinctively to mind. While over all hovers a semitropical atmosphere so apparent that Charleston has been called a West Indian city.

Like other colonials, Charlestonians in the early days built many of their houses of wood, but when repeated fires reduced one after another to ashes, the Assembly forbade the use of this material save for windows, shutters, and interior work. The row after row of brick houses which arose in response to this law would have made Charleston a somber place had not their owners lent a touch of southern color by stuccoing them over in shades of pink, green, yellow, and blue. The picturesque effect was heightened by the pink and purple tiles, whose curving surfaces gave a softness to the roofs in sharp contrast to the hardness of the slate or shingles in use elsewhere.

It was inevitable that this quaint old Charleston, the Charleston of Isaac Mazÿck, Colonel William Rhett, and Arthur Mid-

[2] Frederick P. Bowes, The Intellectual Life of Early Charleston, MS., p. 10.

dleton, should give way to a newer Charleston built in the prevailing English Georgian style. Wealthy Charlestonians, whether merchants or planters, whether of English or Huguenot or West Indian descent, by this time were under the cultural dominance of London, and when one of them visited the mother country he acquired a contempt for the old houses of his father and grandfather and returned with the determination to build after the "modern taste." Perhaps he brought with him in his luggage a book or two on architecture. But this was not essential, for he could easily find an architect, perhaps an Englishman, perhaps a Charlestonian trained in England, capable of designing houses in the Georgian style.[3]

It was not an easy matter, however, to adapt this style to the narrow building lots of the city, the climate, and to the customs of the people. The very essence of the Georgian was the balanced façade, the exactly spaced windows, and especially the classical door with its Ionic or Doric columns, ornate pediment, and stone steps. Charlestonians were unwilling to sacrifice the double- or triple-decked piazza to make room for these features, while it was difficult to have them on the narrow end of the house fronting on the street. The problem was solved in a unique, though not very satisfactory, way, by retaining the piazza, placing the pediment above it, and building a partition in it on the street end in which was placed an ornate door. These sham doors so unique in architecture have become a distinguishing feature of the Charleston Georgian single house. Many in themselves are things of beauty, for upon them the builders lavished their greatest care, but the effect is not pleasing, for they throw the entire facade out of balance. It is as though a man wore his necktie on his shoulder or the mast of a ship arose from the gunwales.

[3] *South Carolina Gazette*, April 29–May 6, 1751.

More in keeping with the Georgian spirit was the so-called double house, typified by the Miles Brewton house, famous alike for its beauty and its part in history. The owner here entertained Josiah Quincy in 1777 and Sir William Campbell two years later, and here Sir Henry Clinton made his headquarters after Brewton had fled with his family never to be heard of again. The porch, with its marble stairs, its stone pillars, its Ionic capitals, its lovely cornices carved by Ezra Waite, is striking in its beauty. Within, the wide hall, the mahogany staircase, the rear Palladian window, the fluted pilasters of the woodwork, the heavy frieze, the marble mantels, the spacious apartments give an impression of dignity, balance, and refined taste which make this house the gem of the city. Certainly the Carolina Georgian, typified by this old mansion, vied with the New England Georgian, or the Philadelphia Georgian, or the Annapolis Georgian in stateliness and beauty.[4]

Above the picturesque roofs of modern Charleston rise two church towers, whose pilasters, arched windows, cornices, and graceful spires speak forcibly of the influence of Sir Christopher Wren. Apparently the South Carolina clergy, unlike their brethren in Virginia, thought that God could be worshiped with as great propriety in a classical as in a Gothic building. The first St. Philip's, which was built in 1682, was replaced forty years later by a building which was called the handsomest church in America. "It has three aisles, an organ and a gallery all round," said a visitor. "The steeple rises octagonal, with windows in each face of the second course ornamented with Ionic pilasters, whose entablature supports a balustrade, from this the tower still rises octagonal, with sashed windows on every other face, till it is terminated by a

[4] A. R. H. Smith and D. E. H. Smith, *The Dwelling Houses of Charleston* (Philadelphia: J. B. Lippincott, 1917), pp. 93–100; *The White Pine Series*, XIV, pp. 219, 220.

dome, upon which stands a lantern for the bells."[5] The building was burned in 1835, and was replaced by a third St. Philip's, which has remained to the present day.

St. Michael's, built in 1752, is patterned after St. Martins-in-the-Fields, London, the notice in the *South Carolina Gazette*, which states that it was "built on the plan of one of Mr. Gibson's plans," undoubtedly referring to James Gibbs. Within and without the church is a product of the Renaissance. The tower, which rises through the roof high above the Doric portico, the recessed choir with its vaulted ceiling and Corinthian pilasters, its beautiful cornice, the arched windows all proclaim its kinship to the Wren school. Breaking sharply with the early traditions of the city, without a trace of West Indian or Huguenot influence, St. Michael's is a bit of Georgian London transplanted in America.[6]

If the occasional English visitor to Charleston was surprised to find that the Georgian style of architecture was so highly in favor, he must have felt even more at home when he entered one of the new residences and found it furnished throughout with the latest and finest Chippendale tables, chairs, and cabinets, some of which were imported from London, some made by local craftsmen. The furniture which graced the Brewton house and Drayton Hall would have fitted exactly into the atmosphere of Berkeley Square. In fact, many of the Charleston craftsmen received their training in England, and such well-known workers as John Fisher, Thomas Lining, William Lupton, James McClellan, and Richard McGrath proudly proclaimed themselves as "lately from London." An exception was Josiah Claypoole, who came to Charleston from Phil-

[5] Mrs. St. Julien Ravenel, *Charleston* (New York: The Macmillan Company, 1906), pp. 97–99.

[6] George S. Holmes, *Historic Sketch of St. Michael's* (Charleston, 1887).

adelphia, but even he, when the rush of orders made it necessary for him to increase his staff, sent in haste for "two good workmen from London."[7]

The Charleston cabinetmakers included in their work almost every kind of furniture, some of it requiring the greatest art in design and a high degree of skill in execution. Claypoole made desks and bookcases with arched, pediment, and O. G. heads, chests of drawers fluted and plain, all sorts of tea tables, sideboards, and waiters, "with the greatest neatness and accuracy."[8] James McClellan made "cabinets, desks and bookcases, bureaus, tables of all sorts, chairs, tea-boxes and new-fashioned chests." Richard McGrath, when he moved from the city put on sale "half a dozen carved chairs, a couch to match them, with commode fronts and pin-cushion seats, of the newest fashion," besides elbow chairs, sofas "made up in the genteelest manner," double chests of drawers, half chests, etc.[9] When what is left of the work of the colonial Charleston cabinetmakers is identified and properly studied, it is probable that much of it will be found to compare favorably with that of northern craftsmen, even the famous Philadelphia artists in wood.

The cabinetmakers had a measure of protection from English competition because of the high cost of freight for such bulky articles as tables and chests of drawers, but the silversmiths were not so favored. Consequently had one entered the dining room of a Charleston mansion prior to the Revolution he might have seen stored away in a Claypoole cupboard, or gracing a McGrath table, a display of silver teapots, por-

[7] *South Carolina Gazette*, April 9–16, 1741, No. 373.

[8] A. C. Prime, *Arts and Crafts in Philadelphia, Maryland, and South Carolina* (Topsfield, Mass.: Wayside Press, 1933), p. 163.

[9] *Ibid.*, p. 175.

ringers, and candlesticks made in London. Yet there were local silversmiths who not only repaired broken pieces, but did creative work. Charles Harris, "working silversmith from London," made "all sorts of new fashioned bottle stands, table-spoons feathered on the handle, dish stands, cruet frames . . . pepper casters, ink stands, mugs, tankards, fluted and plain turin ladles," etc.[10]

Though wealthy Charlestonians filled their houses with fine furniture and fine silver, few seem to have realized the decorative possibilities of fine paintings. Rare indeed was it for one of them to visit Rome or even Paris, so that the works of the great masters were unknown to them and their interest in painting was limited, until the period just prior to the Revolution, to portraiture, or "face painting" as they called it. When a Manigault or a Brewton went abroad on business or to attend college, he often seized the opportunity to have some distinguished artist paint his likeness, and brought it proudly home to decorate his Charleston residence. Benjamin West made portraits of Arthur Middleton with his wife and child, of Thomas Middleton, and Ralph Izard. Izard was painted also by John Zoffany and John Singleton Copley, Mrs. Izard by both West and Gainsborough, Miles Brewton by Sir Joshua Reynolds, Peter Manigault by Allan Ramsay.[11]

Nor was Charleston without its own portrait painters. Of these the best known was Jeremiah Theus, who was at work in his studio on Market Square as early as 1740 and continued until his death thirty-four years later.[12] No less than forty Theus portraits have been listed, among them paintings of

[10] *Ibid.*, p. 67.

[11] Edward McCrady, *Education in South Carolina* (Charleston, S. C.: Historical Society of South Carolina), Appendix, pp. 51–54.

[12] *South Carolina Gazette*, September 6, 1740.

Samuel Prioleau and his wife, Mr. and Mrs. Gabriel Manigault, Peter Porcher, Mrs. Thomas Cordes, and Mr. and Mrs. Manuel Josephson. Although some of Theus's work was attributed formerly to Copley, it lacks the touch of genius which characterized the early portraits of the Bostonian. As William Dunlap says, Theus did not know how to "give grace and picturesque effect to the stiff brocades, enormous ruffles and *outre* stays and stomachers of our grandmothers, or the wigs, velvet coats and waistcoats . . . of our grandfathers." Yet his drawing was accurate and the coloring good. That he was appreciated by his fellow Charlestonians is indicated by the fact that he acquired a considerable fortune, owned a residence at the corner of Broad and Mazÿck Streets, and boasted a pew in St. Michael's.[13]

The interests of the wealthy Charlestonian were by no means entirely centered on material things—his mansion, his Chippendale furniture, his silver, the portraits which adorned his walls. None better than he realized that for the perfect gentleman the cultivation of the mind also was essential. The conversation in the drawing room of the Huger house, or the reception room of the Pringle house, was not confined to politics, or the races, or to Parson Heywood's latest sermon, for the novels of Richardson and Fielding would come in for a share of attention, or perhaps the latest concert, or Hallam's presentation of *Hamlet*, or an article in *The Spectator*, or the latest discoveries in electricity, or the advisability of inoculation for smallpox, or the utility of the ancient languages.

The quest for culture which early brought before the Carolinians the problem of educating their sons and daughters was rendered less difficult than in Virginia and Maryland, because

[13] William Dunlap, *History of Rise and Progress of the Arts of Design in the United States* (Boston: C. E. Goodspeed and Company, 1918), Vol. 1, p. 31.

of the all-important role played by Charleston in the life of the Carolina low country. It was comparatively easy to build up efficient schools when they were patronized not only by the merchants but by the rice and indigo planters as well, who either occupied their town residences during the session or entered their children as boarders. When the rim of settlements was pushed out to the west and north by the founding of Orangeburg and other towns, it became necessary to establish local schools, which labored under the usual difficulties of the frontier, but for the low country Charleston remained the educational, as it was the commercial and social, center.

It was the Anglican missionaries sent over by the Society for the Propagation of the Gospel, who took the lead in establishing schools, though they were effectively seconded by an Act of Assembly in 1712 providing for instruction in "grammar and other arts and sciences and useful learning." A Free School was set up in Charleston and classes begun under a Scotsman from Philadelphia named John Douglass. A decade later the Society sent over as headmaster the Reverend Thomas Morritt, who brought to his task not only enthusiasm, but a plan of study which proved a bit too strenuous for the Carolina youths. They were to start with Latin grammar, continue with composition, and then plunge into Erasmus, Ovid, Virgil, Horace, and Tacitus. In Greek they were to cover Lucian, Isocrates, Hesiod, Homer, and Euripides; while with their "spare time at home" they were to read books on "antiquity."[14]

The Free School, which continued throughout the colonial period, was spurred on to good work by the competition of numerous private schools. Year after year the *Gazette* carried notices of masters who gave instruction in reading, writing, and arithmetic, usually in their residences; or of grammar schools, with courses in Latin, French, geometry, geography,

[14] Frederick P. Bowes, *op. cit.*, p. 56.

history, and perhaps Greek. Despite the influence of the Anglican Church, the chief end of these schools was not preparation for the ministry, or even for a godly life, but for the polite society in which the young must play their part. Young ladies were trained in dancing, music, embroidery, drawing, needlework, and French; boys were early grounded in the classics, French, geography, history, mathematics, physics, and even riding, fencing, and drawing.

On the other hand, it was not forgotten that the young man must some day take over his father's mercantile business or his rice plantation. William Walton expressed a widespread sentiment when he questioned the utility of Latin and Greek to those who were "to spend their days in rural, mercantile or mechanical employments." In his school the emphasis was upon English, arithmetic, bookkeeping, geography, and history.[15] As early as 1733 John Miller had a school in Broad Street where courses were given in arithmetic, algebra, geometry, trigonometry, surveying, navigation, astronomy, the use of the globes, and Italian bookkeeping.[16]

With thoughtful Carolinians it was a matter of deep concern that there was no college within their borders, so that young men aspiring to higher education must go to institutions in other colonies, or perhaps to Oxford or Cambridge or one of the Inns of Court. Over and over again this matter came up for discussion or was aired in the local gazettes. "Was learning thus established and encouraged among us," wrote one correspondent "with what pleasure might our imagination rise with the progress of it . . . and hopes of seeing the bar, the bench and the pulpit honorably filled with the produce of our own province."[17]

[15] *South Carolina Gazette*, October 20, 177[illegible].
[16] *Ibid.*, May 12–13, 1733.
[17] *Ibid.*, March 25–April 1, 1732.

Franklin's appeal for an academy in Philadelphia was read by many in Charleston who pointed out that his reasoning was equally applicable to their province. In a discussion in one of the local clubs it was pointed out that a sufficient endowment might be raised by lottery together with a tax on riding chairs,[18] but once more the opportunity passed, so that when the Revolution overtook South Carolina it was still without any institution of higher learning.

Lacking a local college and distrustful alike of the Calvinist influence of Princeton and Yale and the skepticism which they had heard existed at William and Mary, many Charleston fathers sent their sons to England to complete their education. When Peter Manigault gave instructions in his will that his sons should "receive the most liberal education the province can afford until the age of eighteen" and then go to England to complete the same, he was undoubtedly expressing the ambition of most South Carolina gentlemen. More popular than Oxford and Cambridge, which had fallen low in public estimation at this time both in England and the colonies, were the Inns of Court. As in Virginia, a knowledge of law was considered essential for a gentleman, not only for the conduct of his business affairs, but to prepare him for a prominent part in the government. We are not surprised then to find C. C. Pinckney, John Laurens, John Rutledge, J. J. Pringle, Charles Bull, Joseph Manigault, William Mazÿck, and other Carolinians studying at the Middle Temple; and Gabriel Manigault, Alexander Garden, Thomas Bee, and others at Lincoln's Inn. John Perroneau alone seems to have selected the Inner Temple.[19]

But the Carolina gentleman, despite the requirements of

[18] *Ibid.*, February 12–19, 1750.
[19] Edward McCrady, *op. cit.*, p. 475*n*.

business or of directing the affairs of the plantation, trusted as much to reading as to courses at school and college for the cultivation of his mind. The books in his library he selected partly for utility, partly to meet the demands of a polite society. There were volumes on law; on medicine, to be consulted in case of sickness in his family or among his slaves; on agriculture and gardening; on religion; the works of great English writers—Pope, Addison, Defoe, Swift; copies of *The Tatler*, *The Spectator*, *The Rambler;* books on science, architecture, history, philosophy, commerce. He seems to have been less interested in the classics than was the Virginia planter, possibly because his mercantile instincts demanded a greater emphasis upon utility. Had George Mason or Peyton Randolph paid him a visit they would have embarrassed him deeply when they interspersed their conversation with quotations from Homer or Cicero, but they would have found him quite their equals in his knowledge of law and their superior in mathematics and business.[20]

The interest in reading manifested itself in a rather remarkable way in 1748 when nine merchants, two planters, a schoolmaster, two lawyers, a printer, a doctor, and a peruke maker met to organize the Charleston Library Society.[21] The original intent was to import magazines and pamphlets, but, with the expansion of the membership to one hundred and thirty, a large fund was raised to purchase not only books but philosophical apparatus. Some of the leading men of the city were connected with the Society, so that it became the center of intellectual life in the colony and in part a substitute for a college. On its shelves were volumes on law, religion, philos-

[20] *South Carolina Gazette*, various issues.

[21] *Proceedings* of the South Carolina Historical Association, 1935, pp. 5–6.

ophy, medicine, science, history, commerce, painting, and its influence upon the life and thought of South Carolina can hardly be overestimated.[22]

Clergymen, with the assistance of the Society for Propagating the Gospel, despite their meager salaries, often built up libraries of considerable size. Reverend Henry Heywood left "several hundred volumes of curious books in Hebrew, Greek, Latin, French, Italian, Dutch and English," together with many manuscript "books and papers on chronology and ancient history."[23] Although Mr. Heywood must have been exceptional in his knowledge of languages, his library was not larger than those of other Carolina ministers. Reverend Richard Ludlum left 250 volumes, Reverend James Parker's books were valued at £200, while Robert Betham, Richard Clarke, and others had gathered around them large collections on divinity, history, and the classics. The Carolina clergy, though not creative theologians, were cultured gentlemen, well qualified for religious leadership in the refined atmosphere of Charleston.

As in other provincial towns, the urge to literary production was discouraged by isolation. "Our condition at best is too much like that of a poor country parish, where the good folks are obliged to chew the cud upon a single sermon the whole six days following," complained a writer in the *Gazette*. "Not so fares it with our countrymen at home . . . there one author lives upon the invention of another and one paper engenders another and to read over the produce of a day would be the labor of a week."[24] Nonetheless, there were intellectual stirrings in Charleston, stimulated by a deep apprecia-

[22] Frederick P. Bowes, *op. cit.*, pp. 94–100.
[23] *South Carolina Gazette*, April 15, 1756.
[24] *Ibid.*, February 2, 1733–1734.

tion of Pope and Addison and other English writers and a desire for self-expression in verse.

Typical were the lines sent to the *Gazette* in 1732 by a "fair correspondent."

Who dare affirm my pow'r is weak,
Whilst I instruct the dumb to speak?
And, what's confess'd a greater deed,
Bestow new life upon the dead!
The things most valu'd here below,
To me, their preservation owe
Things past with me as present are.[25]

Somewhat better were "Clio's" lines "On the Omnipresence of The Diety," beginning:

Nature's great God, in every scene is found,
In storms and thunder and in the deep profound;
In clouds and rain that deluge all the land
We view the traces of the Almighty's hand.[26]

One wonders whether Whittier ever stumbled upon an old copy of the *South Carolina Gazette* and there found in a little poem entitled "The Milkmaid" the inspiration for his "Maud Muller."

In the sprightly month of May
When all smells sweet and looks so gay
There tripp'd along a buxom lass
With a milk-pail o'er the grass.[27]

More important than these weak attempts at poetry were the editorials and articles which appeared in the *Gazette*, many of them original, others copied from London papers. In 1732 alone one finds an editorial defending the freedom of the press,

[25] *Ibid.*, January 15–22, 1732.
[26] *Ibid.*, December 17, 1772.
[27] *Ibid.*, February 17, 1733.

an article on the invention of printing, an essay on slander, articles on tanning, the silkworm, and education, and editorials on death, rectitude of mind, and swearing. Under Thomas Whitemarsh and Lewis Timothy the *South Carolina Gazette* was firmly established, and under Timothy's wife Elizabeth and their son Peter it continued for thirty years as a force for literary expression. In the quaint old columns one finds articles on law, science, medicine, and morals printed side by side with export statistics, weather reports, advertisements of general merchandise, medicines, and artisans or, now and then, controversial letters upon religious matters.[28]

Among those who treasured every word of the scientific articles was the unusually large and progressive medical fraternity. Perhaps it was Charleston's reputation for unhealthfulness, the prevalence of malaria, pleurisy, and gout, and the recurring epidemics of yellow fever and smallpox which attracted these men. In an age of medical quacks and when the standards of the profession in the colonies were distressingly low, Charleston could boast of Thomas Dale, William Bull, John Moultrie, Alexander Bacon, Charles Drayton, James Killpatrick, and John Lining, able physicians, all of them. Save for the last named, these men were not creative scientists, but they were well trained in European universities and quick to give their patients the benefits of the latest advances in medical science. Dr. Killpatrick, indeed, was too progressive to suit public opinion, for his advocacy and use of inoculation for smallpox blew up such a storm of protest that he left for London where he earned added distinction in his profession.[29]

[28] Frederick P. Bowes, *op. cit.*, pp. 113–120.

[29] *South Carolina Gazette*, September 14, October 12, 1738, January 25, 1739.

John Lining was not only a physician but a scientist of marked ability. The connection between disease and the weather first claimed his attention, and his long observations, in which he used his own body as the guinea pig, were published in the *Philosophical Transactions* of the Royal Society. He also made a study of yellow fever, without, however, advancing any theory as to its transmission or treatment. Lining's patients must have suffered as a consequence of his scientific interests, for we find him day after day, equipped with a barometer, thermometer, and whipcord hygroscope, recording the temperature and humidity, as well as the rainfall and force of the wind. He found time, also, to investigate the properties of electricity and his repetition of Franklin's kite experiment he describes in a letter published in the *Gentleman's Magazine*.[30]

The practical bent of the Carolinian which made him investigate the causes of the diseases to which the Charleston region was subject explains also his interest in its soil and the possibilities for new and richer products. It was this which gave him his great staple of rice, for the plant was not indigenous to South Carolina, but was brought in, if we may credit tradition, from far-off Madagascar. As it was John Rolfe who gave tobacco to Virginia, so it was the experiments of Dr. Henry Woodward that turned the Carolinians to the cultivation of the crop which was the basis of their future prosperity. Perhaps it was Woodward's example which inspired the experiments with indigo of Ėliza Lucas, the mother of Thomas and Charles Cotesworth Pinckney, and brought a second major product to the Charleston region. Thus it was not the soil alone which made the low country rich, but the intelligent interest of the people in agriculture and their de-

[30] Frederick P. Bowes, *op. cit.*, pp. 133–137.

termination to use to the best advantage what nature had given them.[31]

But while Woodward and Eliza Lucas were making their practical experiments, others were interested in the purely scientific aspects of the flora and fauna of South Carolina. John Lawson was the first to classify and describe the "spontaneous fruits" of the region, together with animals, birds, reptiles, and fish. While in 1722 Mark Catesby gathered material for his volumes on *The Natural History of Carolina*. But the outstanding scientist of colonial South Carolina and the only Carolinian to become a member of the Royal Society was Dr. Alexander Garden, famous for his work in botany and zoölogy. Perhaps very few persons who enjoy the beautiful "gardenia" realize that the great Linnaeus gave it its name as an expression of admiration for this South Carolinian.[32] He it was also who was instrumental in sending the first eels to Europe, and his accounts of his experiments in which a number of persons joining hands received an electrical shock by having contact with the fish were received with astonishment.

The interest in scientific matters found expression in the organization of the Charleston Museum, the first of its kind in America. Here was fitted up a room for the display of specimens and an appeal was sent out for "quadrupeds, birds, fishes, reptiles, insects, worms, etc. with the best accounts of their customs and natural habitudes," as well as for samples of flowers and other plants, fossils, ores, minerals, and shells.[33] The leaders in this movement, most of them, had already shown their devotion to intellectual matters by founding the Library Society, and the Charleston Museum was a further evidence

[31] Harriet H. R. Ravenel, *Eliza Pinckney* (New York: Charles Scribner's Sons, 1896).

[32] Frederick E. Brasch, *op. cit.*, pp. 33–34.

[33] *South Carolina Gazette*, March 22, April 5, 12, 1773.

of the breadth of their interests. Had they crowned their efforts by establishing a college, Charleston would have been one of the most important cultural centers in the colonies.

But neither scientific pursuits nor attention to the demands of the plantation and the countinghouse were enough to wean the Charlestonian from his deep love of the theater, and his attendance at the performances of *Hamlet* or *Cato* he accounted as time spent not only pleasantly but profitably. With the Quaker and Puritan abhorrence of the stage he had no sympathy and at the very first recorded performance in the city there was a pointed and decisive reference in the epilogue to the New England narrowness.

> *Nor real virtue blames the pleasing strife,*
> *To blend amusement with the shades of life;*
> *Wise, innocent, serene, she smiles at ease*
> *Nor hanging witches, nor abjuring plays.*[34]

The opening play, *The Orphan*, was presented in the Court Room, but soon after a regular theater was built in Dock Street, within a hundred yards of St. Philip's, with boxes, pit, and gallery. Here were presented *The Recruiting Officer*, *Cato*, and other popular plays. Although things appear to have gone badly, and the theater was sold early in 1736, we conclude from a notice in the *Gazette* of October 1741, which mentions the "lot of land whereon the theatre now stands," that it continued to be used from time to time.[35] Eight years later, however, when one Stokes, who had "acted on the stage in Dublin, Edinburgh and Goodman's Fields," gave several "dramatic entertainments," he had to use the courtroom at Mrs. Blythe's.[36]

[34] *Ibid.*, February 22, 1735.
[35] October 3, 1741.
[36] *South Carolina Gazette*, November 20–27, 1749.

It was only in 1754, with the arrival from Philadelphia of a company of players, probably the Hallams, that Charlestonians had a real theatrical season.[37] Opening at the "new theatre" with *The Fair Penitent*, the company continued with *A Bold Stroke for a Wife*, *The Orphan*, and *The Recruiting Officer*.[38] After their departure the curtain fell upon the Charleston stage, to remain down for nearly a decade. It was with enthusiasm, then, that in November 1763 the *Gazette* announced that a company of players under David Douglass had arrived from the North, "Where they have performed several years with great applause." A theater had already been contracted for, 75 by 35 feet, and with its completion began a series of performances such as Charleston had never witnessed before—*King Lear*, *The Sham Doctor*, *Romeo and Juliet*, and many others.[39] Douglass was so encouraged by the response of the Charleston public that he made a trip to London to secure "a most excellent set of scenes done by Mr. Doll, principal scene-painter to Covent Garden," together with "some very eminent performers from both theatres in London."[40]

But he was so far from being satisfied with the inadequate size and equipment of the little theater in Queen Street that in 1773 he built a new one which was described as "elegantly furnished" and one of the most commodious on the continent. With the opening performances, *A Word to the Wise* and *High Life Below Stairs*, the audience was delighted with the well-designed scenery, the costumes, the music, and the lighting. During the season no less than forty-eight plays and

[37] The Hallams left Philadelphia in the summer of 1754 for a tour of the West Indies. It seems certain that they made Charleston one of their stopping points.

[38] *South Carolina Gazette*, September 4, October 3, 1754.

[39] *Ibid.*, November 5, 1763.

[40] *Ibid.*, October 31, 1765.

twenty-nine farces were presented, among them *Julius Caesar*, seen for the first time by an American audience, and ten other of Shakespeare's works. This was one of the most brilliant seasons in the history of the colonial stage and went far toward compensating Charlestonians for the theatrical famines of preceding years.[41]

During the long intervals between the appearance of theatrical companies Charlestonians consoled themselves with numerous concerts, some of them given as early as 1732. In such high esteem was music held that the dignified members of the Council thought it no impropriety to lend their hall, although on one occasion the concert was postponed "on account of the Council's sitting."[42] The English and Scottish songs, as well as the instrumental music, were well received by the select audiences, who, after the last strains had died out, often continued the entertainment by using the musicians as a dance orchestra and selecting partners for the minuet or for "country dances."[43]

With this background of musical experience, furthered by a group of competent instructors on the violin, harpsichord, guitar, and flute, Charleston was prepared for the important step of organizing the first musical organization in America, the St. Cecilia Society. Backed by some of the wealthiest men in the colony and well supported by the public, the Society employed the best musicians to be had in America, even advertising in the Boston gazettes for violin, hautboy, and bassoon players.[44] Josiah Quincy was duly impressed. "The music was good—the two bass viols and French horns were grand," he

[41] Arthur Hornblow, *op. cit.*, I, pp. 146, 147.

[42] *South Carolina Gazette*, November 18–25, 1732.

[43] *Ibid.*, October 14–21, 1732.

[44] Oscar G. Sonneck, *Early Concert Life in America* (Leipzig, 1907), pp. 18, 19.

jotted down in his *Journal.* "One Abercrombie, a Frenchman just arrived, played the first violin and a solo incomparably better than any one I ever heard. He cannot speak a word of English and has a salary of five hundred guineas a year from the St. Cecilia Society. There were upwards of two hundred and fifty ladies present, and it was called no great number."[45]

The visitors to Charleston in the decades just preceding the Revolution were fascinated with its unique society. Josiah Quincy, Jr., remarked upon the "richness and elegance" of attire, the sumptuous dinners, the elegance of the architecture, the richness of the interior fittings, the unequal distribution of wealth; the inattention of the people to "political inquiries and philosophic disquisitions," their neglect of the Puritan Sabbath, the fewness of "men of letters and science."[46] This no doubt was the hasty judgment based upon a brief acquaintance only, but it reveals the striking difference between the social capital of the far South and the social capital of New England. To a Bostonian, Charleston seemed strange, indeed, its culture the culture of a foreign people.

The West Indian atmosphere which lingered even in the days when Quincy visited the city, the traces of Huguenot influence, the mingling of the merchant and planter aristocracies in the Charleston drawing rooms, the huge fortunes accumulated in the culture of rice and in the rice trade, the semitropical climate, with its influence upon architecture and daily life, gave to Charleston a unique culture, a culture which would have seemed to Washington or to Charles Carroll almost as unfamiliar as to the New England Puritan. Charleston, of course, like other provincial cities, was clearly under the

[45] Massachusetts Historical Society *Proceedings,* XLIX, "Journal," March 3, 1773.

[46] *Ibid.,* pp. 454–456.

cultural dominance of London and strove to shape its social and intellectual life in conformity with the prevailing trends in the mother country. But despite herself she retained her individuality to the last because she could not ignore her climate and her peculiar economic conditions or forget her traditions.

CONCLUSION

EIGHTEENTH-CENTURY American culture was the culture of contemporaneous England transplanted in America and superimposed upon the various civilizations that had developed there. It had, therefore, a degree of uniformity which was lacking in earlier days. The architecture of Boston in the decades preceding the Revolution had much in common with the architecture of Philadelphia, Annapolis, and Charleston because the English Georgian house, expressed in the books of Gibbs, or Halfpenny, or Ware, was the model for them all. Theatrical productions in one colony were like those in others, since they were produced by the same company of itinerant English actors. There was a uniformity in the work of the colonial cabinetmakers, because they all conformed to the English styles, whether Queen Anne, or Chippendale, or Sheraton.

Yet it was inevitable that the stream of English culture beating against the American shore should be deeply affected by that shore itself, and affected differently in each section. The warm welcome accorded the English theater in the South, the bitter opposition of Philadelphia, the complete ban laid down by New England were but expressions of the different traditions and concepts of these communities. The difference between a Georgian residence on Beacon Hill and on Capitol Green, Williamsburg, was the difference between the climate of Boston and Virginia, building materials, the life of the Bostonian and Virginian. In Massachusetts reading directed itself into the more serious literary channels; in Annapolis the modern novelists enjoyed a great popularity.

Throughout the colonies Georgian culture, with all its elegance, its display of wealth, its beautiful houses, its costly furniture, its growing libraries, was based upon the improvement in education. In the pioneer civilization of the seventeenth century education suffered not only because of the sparseness of the population, but because of the duplication which resulted from the insistence of each religious denomination upon having its own educational system. When a rural community of a hundred or so scattered families tried to set up four or five schools, one run by the Quakers, another by the Episcopalians, another by the Presbyterians, another by the Dutch Reformed, none would be efficient.

But with the growth of population and wealth, and the development of commercial cities in the eighteenth century, the situation became more favorable. Private schools were established which were nondenominational. The famous William Penn Charter School, the two town grammar schools in Boston, the Annapolis Free School, and many others were equal to some of the best in England. As for the various Presbyterian academies, modeled upon the dissenting academies of England, which were a combination of classical school and theological seminary, their work was remarkably thorough. Out from Samuel Blair's academy at Fagg's Manor, Pennsylvania, from Samuel Finley's academy at Nottingham, Maryland, from Jonathan Dickinson's school at Elizabeth, and especially from the so-called Log College went some of the ablest ministers in America.

With the multiplying of the preparatory schools, there came a demand for the founding of additional colleges. In New England Harvard and Yale had long monopolized the field, while William and Mary was the only college west and south of the Hudson. But in the mid-eighteenth century one new college after the other opened its doors—Princeton, the

University of Pennsylvania, Columbia, Rutgers, Brown, Dartmouth, Hampden-Sydney, etc. These institutions, most of them, were founded by various denominational sects, chiefly for the purpose of training young men for the ministry, but they also sent out hundreds of laymen to take leading roles in the social, economic, and political life of the colonies. Despite the stream of wealthy boys from America to the English universities, life in Williamsburg, or Boston, or Philadelphia would have been less polished had it not been for the rapid expansion of education at the college level which marked the third quarter of the century.

At the same time, one wonders whether reading was not an even more important factor. For one youth who went to college there were scores who had the opportunity to purchase books or to join one of the circulating libraries. The increase in reading was the result of the accumulation of wealth and of better schools rather than of cheaper books, for modern printing presses had not been invented and the type was set by hand. It is true that paper-back novels could be had for one shilling, sixpence, but an edition of Shakespeare cost as much in 1775 as in 1700. Yet the ships from England each year brought thousands of volumes to the colonies and the bookstores in all the larger towns were crowded with works on religion, history, science, medicine, law, philosophy, architecture, agriculture, as well as the classics, drama, poetry, and fiction.

The centers of colonial culture had no way of shaping the character of English literature except in so far as they added to the purchasing public, but they expressed their individuality by their selections. The Annapolis gentlemen, taking their reading rather lightly, steeped themselves in fiction and the drama, shied off from works on theology, and searched Cicero and Horace chiefly for quotations for witty sallies; the Bostonian, wincing under the warnings of the clergy that fiction was a harmful mental dissipation, read his Fielding or his Richardson with a guilty conscience, to be atoned for only by more copious doses of theology or books on piety; the Virginian read the classics to round out his education as a gentleman and Coke and Locke to equip himself for a place in the colonial government, salving his conscience with Bishop Tillotson's works or perhaps *The Whole Duty of Man.*

In architecture, even more than in reading, the individuality of American centers expressed itself. If one transplants the seed of Havana tobacco in the Connecticut valley, in Pennsylvania, and in North Carolina, one will get a different leaf in each place, each differing also from the parent leaf. So it was with the Georgian architecture which conquered America in the eighteenth century and in turn was conquered by America. When Robert Smith and Dr. William Shippen sat down together to plan Nassau Hall, they certainly spread out before them various English books of architecture and decided upon one design which they considered most suited to their needs. But they then so modified it as to make it almost unrecognizable—by removing marble balustrades and pediments, since marble was not available at Princeton, substituting rough stone for cut stone or brick, adding a simple cupola taken from the tower of St. Mary-le-Strand. When the building was completed there was no difficulty in recognizing it as Georgian in style, yet there was nothing like it in England, nor even in Boston or Charleston. It belonged to New Jersey, or possibly Pennsylvania, as unmistakably as the Delaware River.

The colonial stage, on the other hand, was far more uniform, since it was almost entirely in the hands of English companies who traveled from town to town. One year they might present a series of plays in New York, the next in Philadelphia, the next at Charleston, the same actors taking the same roles. Had these places developed their own talent, had their literary lights written plays for local presentation, the colonial theater might have been as diverse as architecture, might have reflected the individuality of each cultural center. As it was, tradition expressed itself only in hostility or cordiality to the stage. Whereas Williamsburg and Annapolis welcomed the drama and feted the actors and actresses, Boston turned a cold shoulder on all that pertained to the stage.

In painting, the cultural dominance of the mother country tended not only to shape the work of native Americans, but actually to convert them into Englishmen. When West, Copley, and Peale went to England for study, they should have confined their efforts to mastering the technique of their art, while clinging stubbornly to their American tradition, with its simplicity, democracy, optimism, and even crudeness. But West and Copley were induced to turn their backs on America and devote themselves to becoming English artists, painting in the current English style, and taking subjects sanctioned by English critics. As a result, West lost his chance for permanent fame and Copley steadily deteriorated. On the other hand, Peale, whose independent spirit would not bow to dictation, probably left England too soon, for he never mastered the technique which might have made him a great painter.

We can only regret that the spirit of colonial America failed to find reflection on the canvases of its native artists. There was an unlimited opportunity. The Indians—their life, their habits, their wars; the vast forest with its wild life, hunters, and silent majestic beauty; the great tobacco fields of the South, the slaves at work, the English ships at anchor in the rivers or tied up at the wharves, the shallow boats laden with tobacco hogsheads, hastening down the upper courses of the streams, the gay assemblages at Westover or Tulip Hill; the busy scenes in the northern harbors, the rapt assemblages that listened to Whitefield and Tennent. Instead, the colonial heritage consists of little more than portraits, some of them invaluable for their revelation of the men and women who lived in America two centuries ago, but most of them lifeless and wooden.

In music there was both uniformity and diversity; both independence and servility. In the cultural centers, where sophisticated audiences assembled in concert halls to listen to trained soloists, or to the opera, or to orchestras, there was a strict conformity to European standards. It was the music of Handel or Bach or Corelli, rendered upon instruments popular in Europe, which was in vogue in Boston as well as Charleston or Williamsburg, and one listened in vain for a song expressive of the American spirit. Yet when the concert was over and the fashionably dressed men and women reached home, they might hear truly American music, perhaps from the cook who sang at her work, perhaps from the stable boy, perhaps from the nurse who sang the children to sleep.

Like other phases of American culture, the ballad came originally from Europe. It is probable that some arrived at Jamestown with Captain Newport in 1607, that others found their way to New England with the Pilgrims; we know that they were brought in by indentured workers, by artisans, by merchants, that they were sung by the Maine fisherman as well as the planter in the tobacco field, by the humble servant maid, and the proud dame. From the master or mistress or from poor whites the Negro slave took up the ballad, adding much of his own distinctive spirit, and giving it a new flavor instantly recognizable, a flavor perhaps leading back to Africa itself.[1] But the whites, too, transformed the ballads, adding here, eliminating there, until they became more American than European. They became expressive, also, not only of life in the New World, but of life in distinctive colonies or sections.

In the artistic crafts we have the same story. From Boston to Charleston there was a uniform subserviency to the dictates of the English masters. When Chippendale was in vogue in London, the American cabinetmaker who dared to make a table or a chair in some other style was apt to have it left on his hands. A highboy made in Philadelphia would fit perfectly into the Hammond House in Annapolis, while a secretary made by Shaw in Annapolis would not have been out of place in Boston, on the one hand, or Charleston, on the other. Nonetheless, any one who knew furniture could have identified the Hammond House highboy as the work of Savery or Randolph, or the secretary as a Shaw piece, even in far-off South Carolina or New England. Had the colonies been suddenly cut off from England, had no more books on cabinetmaking been available, had there been no further imports of furniture, each colonial cultural center would probably have developed styles of its own; instead of a Philadelphia Sheraton or a Newport Chippendale, we might have had pure Philadelphian, or pure Newport. As it was, what we had was Queen Anne, or Chippendale, or Sheraton, or Hepplewhite, with a Newport, or a New York, or a Philadelphia flavor.

One could wish that colonial culture as expressed in literature, music, the theater, the artistic crafts had been more democratic and less aristocratic, more American and less English. But it was wealth that made it possible, so it is natural

[1] It would seem unfortunate that in editing some of the spirituals musical writers have only too often eliminated the Negro flavor, thus leaving the form without the spirit.

that it should be expressive of the life of the wealthy. The recent awakening of America to the richness of its cultural heritage has been accompanied by a commendable effort to preserve what time has left to us of old buildings, books, furniture, silverware, pewter, etc. Today a Philadelphia highboy is worth a small fortune; Stratford, Carter's Grove, the Hammond House, Mount Pleasant have been restored; in Williamsburg a whole village, with its buildings, gardens, furniture, music, has been brought back to life as by the touch of a magician's wand; the American wing of the Metropolitan Museum of Art has been a revelation to many thousands of the good taste of our ancestors as well as of the luxury with which some of them surrounded themselves.

INDEX